The Antarctic Dive Guide

Third Edition
Fully Revised and Updated

Lisa Eareckson Kelley

For Dennis

WILDGuides

PRINCETON

press.princeton.edu

Published by Princeton University Press,
41 William Street, Princeton, New Jersey 08540
In the United Kingdom: Princeton University Press, 6 Oxford Street,
Woodstock, Oxfordshire OX20 1TW
nathist.press.princeton.edu

Requests for permission to reproduce material from this work should be sent to
Permissions, Princeton University Press

First published 2006 by **WILD**_Guides_ Ltd.
Second Edition 2008 by **WILD**_Guides_ Ltd.
Third Edition 2015

British Library Cataloging-in-Publication Data is available

Library of Congress Control Number 2014949506
ISBN 978-0-691-16344-4

Production and design by **WILD**_Guides_ Ltd., Old Basing, Hampshire UK.

Printed in China

10 9 8 7 6 5 4 3 2 1

CONTENTS

ACKNOWLEDGEMENTS

The Antarctic is a relatively new location for recreational Scuba Diving, and in the few years that it has been a taking place, a few individuals have pioneered the techniques, explored the region for the best sites, and amassed a wealth of knowledge. This guide is an attempt to share this information, allowing more divers to experience this amazing underwater habitat, and would not have been possible without the knowledge and generous contributions of both text and photographs from the following: Dennis Cornejo, David Cothran, Toni Davis, Denise Landau of IAATO, Shona Muir (BAS) and the Kirsty Brown Fund, Göran Ehlmé, Henrik Enckell, Martin Enckell, Debbie Harrison, Kim Heacox, Tony Soper, Oscar Johansson, John Durban and Bob Pitman, Bill Baker, Jen Hayes and David Doubilet, and Paul Nicklen.

Thanks to those that pushed me to write the book, Rob Still and Andy Swash at **WILD**Guides for taking on such an unusual project, and the following people for never-ending support, advice and even text editing: Henrik Ahlberg, Trey Byus, Kim Crosbie, Matt Drennan, Amanda, and the entire Ellerbeck family, Richard Butler, Marlynda Elstgeest and Waterproof Expeditions, Melanie Heacox, Bob Houston, Brent Houston, Eleanor, Norman, and the entire Murray Family, Ron Naveen, Jack Putnam, Jim and Chris Sanders, Richard Schager, Roff Smith, Hilary Soper, Patrik Svärdmyr and Jason Kelley. A very special thanks to Tim Soper for the hours of assistance and editing he has put into this book.

Diving and photographing in these waters has been made much more comfortable and effective thanks to good advice and equipment from: Backscatter Underwater Video and Photography, Diving Unlimited International (DUI), and the Monterey Bay Dive Center.

I was introduced to this amazing underwater world while working aboard the expedition vessels *National Geographic Endeavour* and *National Geographic Explorer*. Captains Karl Lampe, Leif Skog and Oliver Kruess' enthusiasm and support of the diving operations is hugely appreciated, as are the members of the deck crew who brave whatever weather mother nature throws at them when they sit in Zodiacs as our life lines on the surface. Thanks to the *Endeavour* and *Explorer* diving crew: my instructor Dennis Cornejo and dive buddies David Cothran, Eugen Kanjski, Tommi Kotilainen, Göran Persson, Tove Peterson, Michael Westelius, Anders Von Hofsten, Jesper Westermark, Max Westman, Magnus Hååard, Dino Udović, Mauro Grl and Oscar Johansson.

None of this would have been possible without Lindblad National Geographic Expeditions, which strives to show its guests every possible aspect of Antarctica, including the underwater realm. It was through Sven Lindblad's continuing commitment to undersea exploration and conservation that I was able to learn to dive, and Antarctica's icy realm revealed.

A BRIEF HISTORY OF DIVING IN ANTARCTICA

The first dive in Antarctica was made in 1902 by Willy Heinrich, the carpenter on Drygalski's 1901–03 expedition. He used a large brass Siebe diving helmet, stiff canvas suit, and heavy lead boots, while supplied with air from the surface. Utilizing this elementary diving gear, Heinrich was able to dive under Drygalski's expedition vessel *Gauss* while she was frozen in the ice, carrying out ship repairs such as caulking of the hull. Heinrich was the pioneer of Antarctic diving, and one of the few divers to explore under the sea ice. Most of his diving peers chose the less risky option of staying in open water due to known problems with safely accessing and exploring under the frozen sea.

It was not until 1946 during the US Navy's pioneering visit to Antarctica, 'Operation High Jump,' that diving became widely publicized. During this operation, divers went down to conduct fuel pipeline inspections, and one document even mentions repair of the submarine *Stennet* near the Ross Ice Shelf. However, despite being much more common place, diving still involved the cumbersome affair of suiting up in a heavy dry suit and large brass helmet, supplied by air either from the surface or a primitive re-breather system.

Through the 1950s diving continued to be an awkward project, and although scientists and navy personnel from both the United States and Australia occasionally used diving to collect underwater specimens, it was not the preferred practice. The scientists who did endeavor to dive for specimens, did so from shore, using bulky gear that made conducting the necessary work difficult and exhausting, causing a realization that the actual gain was not worth the effort.

Finally, in 1961 a breakthrough was made: the first open circuit SCUBA (self-contained underwater breathing apparatus) dive was made in McMurdo Sound. In conjunction with a project to test a sea ice eroding device called the 'Aqua Therm,' Jim Thorne and Donald Johnson made one dive. They used the newest advancement in dry suits, moving away from the old stiff suits, and opting for a more flexible version. These new dry suits had rubberized neck seals and allowed compressed air to be pumped into the suit for an extra layer of warmth.

Diving equipment has progressed monumentally from early surface supplied air dives to today's SCUBA

In 1962, Philip Law, director of the Australian National Antarctic Research Expedition (ANARE), brought down the newest generation of dry and wet suits, along with an early version of the standard SCUBA gear that is used today. The large brass helmet was done away with, and newer more comfortable alternatives were tried. For a period of time divers tried using the full face mask to avoid having the frigid water touch their faces, but found that due to flooding, equalization difficulties, and the lack of buddy-breathing capabilities, the regular mask and mouthpiece were the best option.

It was during the 1961–62 season that Verne E. Peckham became the first person to dive extensively under the Antarctic ice. Peckham set the standards for today's under ice diving by using a chainsaw to cut a hole into the ice, then covering it with a hut to provide

The first SCUBA diving in Antarctica took place below the ice in McMurdo Sound during the 1960s

shelter when entering and exiting the water. He used a dry suit with integrated gloves, and was tethered to the surface while moving beneath the ice. Also the first person to conduct scientific diving, Peckham studied the benthic ecology, which included collecting specimens for terrestrial tank observation and creating marked underwater observational sites for long-term research.

From this point onward, dives in Antarctica became more frequent for both scientific and governmental agencies. It was also during this time that the first formal diving rules were set in place by the United States Antarctic Program (USAP). James Stewart drafted the first scientific diving rules in 1967, which included always diving with a buddy, and having a dive tender on the surface.

It is through the trial and error of our Antarctic diving forefathers, such as Willy Heinrich, that we have made such technological advancements in diving. Today we dive with dry suits that offer as much mobility as our everyday clothing, and have developed communication devices that allow us to talk to the surface while underwater.

Seeing the progress that has been made in the last 100 years, not to mention the last 40, leads me to believe that in another 40 years it will be we who look as though we are diving in the stone ages.

Diving in Antarctica has developed from a rare and sensational project, to an everyday occurrence during the austral summer.

THE CONTINENT OF ANTARCTICA

Overview

Around 200 million years ago Antarctica was joined with Australia, Africa, South America, India, and New Zealand, as part of the supercontinent of Gondwana. As tectonic plates groaned and shifted across the globe, Gondwana began to break apart, its pieces creating the continents and islands we know today. Settling into its south polar position, Antarctica began to cool rapidly. The world's fifth largest continent, Antarctica's 13·9 million square kilometers feature massive mountain ranges, hills, valleys, and plains. The continent's present shape has been best described as a 'stingray', the tail pointing towards South America's Tierra Del Fuego, and the head towards the Indian Ocean. Antarctica's most remarkable feature however, is that 98% of its landmass is covered in ice, measuring 4,775 m thick in some places. Additionally, the continent effectively doubles in size as sea ice extends up to 1,000 km from the coast during the Antarctic winter.

Although Antarctica's political boundary encompasses everything below 60° S, the environmental boundary of the Antarctic Convergence is considered the true start of Antarctic ecology. The convergence occurs as the cooler southern ocean waters meet those of the warmer northern oceans. Here this interface acts as a mixing agent, bringing an upwelling of nutrients to the surface. Although the water surrounding the Antarctic rarely gets above the freezing point, it is some of the most nutrient rich in the world, creating a thriving environment for creatures large and small.

History

Like many lands in ancient history, Antarctica was hypothesized to exist before it was actually discovered, and reports dating back as far as 650AD proclaimed a great area of frozen land in the south. Exploration exploded in the 1400s, as explorers began to investigate the most southerly latitudes, searching for new routes to India and South America. During this time, incredible revelations were made about the size, shape, and diversity of our planet. Alas, due to the extreme weather conditions of our southern oceans and unreliable navigation techniques, the great southern continent, known then as *Terra Australis Incognita*, continued to elude explorers for many centuries.

Sailors and explorers continued the search for the great white continent without success, a prime example being Captain James Cook in 1773, who despite pushing well below the Antarctic circle to 70° S, was stopped by a barrier of sea ice and never sighted land. On the other hand, when Bellinghausen became the first person to glimpse land in 1820, his splendid efforts in conquering this southern enigma went largely unnoticed by the industrial world. It was not until the advent of commercial sealing and whaling in the late 1700s that exploration became a sustainable business. As the sealers and whalers devoured the marine mammal populations and looked further into the most southern reaches of the ocean for more viable resources, they also made the first surveys and charts of Antarctica.

Having thoroughly investigated the accessible shoreline, by the early 1900s many expeditions were being sent to explore the interior of the white continent. The first overwintering ashore took place on Cape Adare in the Ross Sea, as part of the British Southern Cross Expedition of 1898–1900, led by Carsten Borchgrevink. Explorers and entrepreneurs flocked to Antarctica in the following years, and the more they learned, the more intriguing this last continent became. They were attracted to the continent for personal, nationalistic, and monetary gain, often creating disputes over the sovereignty of a location. These explorations of the heroic era were rife with tragedy and triumph, and many lives were lost between the glories of discovery.

Tourism

Tourism in Antarctica dates back as early as Thomas Cook (1910) and J.R. Stenhouse (1929), its early roots beginning with the Falkland Island Dependancies Government using a mail steamer to take a limited number of passengers annually from the Falkland Islands to South Georgia, as well as the South Orkney and South Shetland Islands. The first dedicated tourist operation occurred on 22 December 1956, when a Douglas DC 6B aircraft of Argentina's Linea Aérea Nacional took 66 passengers on a four-hour scenic flight over the Antarctic Peninsula and adjacent islands.

Antarctica's harsh environment is sure to conjure up ideas of intrepid explorers weathering blistering snowstorms, so it is not surprising that early tourism to the continent was completely expeditionary in nature. With few opportunities, and requiring long and sometimes difficult travel, it remained an adventure that few took the opportunity to enjoy. This all changed in 1966 when Lars Eric Lindblad pioneered the first regular Antarctic expedition cruises. Suddenly, an everyday person could travel to the bottom of the world, experiencing at first-hand what once had only been seen on television, or read about in books and magazines. Using the purpose-built expedition ship, *Lindblad Explorer,* equipped with small inflatable boats called Zodiacs, visitors were transported to the Antarctic Peninsula on voyages lasting about two weeks. Such voyages took place several times during the summer season.

This small venture started an explosive trend; currently (2014) there are 42 ships or yachts that visit the white continent each summer season, and as many as 35,000 tourists call on the continent each year on yachts, ships, planes and inland expeditions. Today, as tourism in Antarctica becomes more commonplace, expedition activities have diversified from traditional Zodiac landings to more extreme adventures such as camping, kayaking, and diving. Although the type and style of travel has evolved, what drives those who visit has changed little from the days of Shackleton, the desire to investigate the unknown.

The Antarctic tourist season is short, only four months between November and March. This is the austral summer, breeding season, and the ideal time of year to catch the wildlife at its peak, while enjoying up to 20 hours of daylight. Every person has different reasons for going to Antarctica; for some it may be the chance to set foot on the 7th continent, others wish to see penguins in their natural habitat, and, for those of you reading this book, the desire to dive or otherwise experience the underwater realm is the attraction.

Underwater

Underwater benthos in Antarctica remains similar throughout the year. However, the underwater visibility varies drastically both during and between the seasons; the best visibility is found in the winter and early spring before the ice breaks up, releasing trapped plankton and nutrients. Currently tourist diving in the Antarctic is limited to the summer months only, when increasing sunlight and warming waters result in plankton blooms. Although this limits visibility, and despite at times not being able to see more than three meters ahead, a diver can still enjoy spectacular benthos.

The Lemaire Channel – one of the most scenic passages in Antarctica

Recreational Scuba diving in Antarctica is a very specialized form of tourist travel, only becoming available in the last two decades. Before this, diving in the Antarctic was the exclusive realm of scientific programs and journalists. Of the 35,000 people who currently visit the continent each year, divers make up a very small percentage. However, Antarctica is fast becoming the world's number one extreme dive destination, and each year the number of divers grows. Organized dive travel to Antarctica is currently limited to a few expedition companies and charter boats, but this is enough to give you several choices for planning your perfect trip. Getting to Antarctica for diving is not the simplest nor the cheapest vacation to choose, so it is important to plan carefully, asking yourself certain questions before you invest in this once in a lifetime experience: What means of travel – ship or yacht? Do I want to enjoy land activities as well as diving? How many people do I want to travel with? How much money can I afford to spend? How long can I be on vacation? The section below aims to give you some insight into your options, and help you make a more informed choice.

Choosing your dive expedition

The majority of tourism takes place in two distinct regions of Antarctica. The Ross Sea sector, south of New Zealand and Australia, is the least visited of the two, with as few as 500 passengers traveling there a year. A much longer sea journey is required to reach this coast and sea ice conditions are more challenging. Therefore few companies run voyages here.

The South American sector is by far the most visited, and where the majority of tourist dive activities take place. South of Argentina and Chile, this sector encompasses the Antarctic Peninsula, South Shetland, and South Sandwich Islands.

Antarctic tourism is ever evolving, and travelers now have a wide variety of means to get to the continent, as well as options of what to do there, choosing from scenic overflights, inland expeditions, or travel by ship. Over 95% of all tourist travel to Antarctica is by sea, and all diving trips use this mode of transportation. Voyages to the Antarctic Peninsula generally take 10–21 days, and the longer voyages may also include South Georgia and the Falkland Islands. The two main ports of departure are Ushuaia in Argentina and Punta Arenas in Chile, although trips may also leave from Stanley, Falkland Islands.

With over 80 operators and 42 ships to choose from, deciding which company to travel with can be a mind-boggling experience. The majority of these companies are members of the International Association of Antarctic Tour Operators (IAATO). IAATO is a member organization founded in 1991 to advocate, promote, and practice safe and environmentally responsible private-sector travel to the Antarctic. Beginning as a assembly of 7 companies, IAATO now has 69 members encompassing ship-operators, land-based operators, ship agents, travel agents, one governmental office, and travel companies that charter planes and ships. Through extensive procedures and guidelines, IAATO has helped to ensure safe environmental practice, appropriate numbers of passengers on shore, site-specific guidelines, and documentation of activities in Antarctica. The member companies have a continued commitment to education through exploration of Antarctica, and recognize the potential environmental impacts that the increasing numbers of tourists to Antarctica can have. Each have endeavored to set the highest possible industry standards. I recommend researching anyone who is not an IAATO member diligently, but ultimately the company and ship you choose largely depends on what kind of activities they offer, the level of service and comfort you are looking for, as well as personal preference.

Ships sailing to Antarctica are split into four categories:

LARGE CRUISE SHIPS (SIGHTSEEING ONLY)

The largest ships, carrying up to 2,000 passengers, merely cruise to Antarctica, spending one or two days sailing through some of the more scenic areas before heading north again, usually to continue along the coast of South America. These ships make no landings, and offer the more traditional cruise ship experience, with food available around-the-clock, casinos, and shows. There are, however, usually one or two guest lectures who travel on these ships to talk about different aspects of Antarctica.

SMALL CRUISE SHIPS

This category encompasses smaller vessels that have a limit of 500 passengers. Three or four landings are usually made at specific sites during a voyage, but since a maximum of 100 passengers is allowed onshore at any given time, each group is only able to spend a short period ashore during each landing.

EXPEDITION SHIPS

Small vessels carrying fewer than 200 passengers are known as expedition ships. Their small size allows their itinerary to be more flexible, making many landings throughout the trip, sometimes as many as 3 a day. As with all ships in the Antarctic, only 100 passengers are allowed ashore at one time, but even with 200 people aboard, there is plenty of time to explore and enjoy Antarctica. These are the only ships to offer diving to their passengers.

Voyages to the Antarctic Peninsula usually last between 8 and 13 days, with 3–10 days actually spent around the peninsula. Two days down and two days back will be spent in the Drake Passage. This crossing is dreaded by many people, as they may have heard stories of tumultuous seas. Often these accounts are exaggerated, but nevertheless this body of water can certainly cause even the largest ship to move side to side and up and down, so be prepared. All ships will try and make the crossing as smooth as possible, but if you are prone to sea-sickness be sure to bring whatever medication works best for you to avoid being ill.

Although expeditionary in name and nature, these ships tend to offer many comforts, such as à la carte meals, cabin service, and naturalist 'expedition staff' who are your guides during landings, and are always on hand to answer questions. Inflatable boats called Zodiacs are the main mode of transportation off the vessel, although a special circumstance may allow the ship to drop the gangway and let passengers walk out onto steady sea ice.

Most expedition ship operators offering a dive program do so in conjunction with a program for non-divers. Generally there are only 8 to 12 divers with 1 or 2 dive masters onboard, so activities are arranged with the land-oriented passengers in mind. On a journey

Divers being assisted after surfacing from a dive.

like this, divers usually have the opportunity to dive once a day during the voyage, allowing them to experience the best of the underwater world as well terrestrial Antarctica.

YACHTS

The last option, and one commonly catering to divers, is a sailing yacht carrying between 8 and 40 passengers. In many cases, especially with the smaller vessel (8–12 people), an entire voyage may be dedicated to diving, but on occasion divers may be on board with land-oriented tourists. Because these trips are in small vessels, jointly wind and motor powered, the trips are longer, lasting between 21 and 37 days. Often a passenger will be part of the working crew, learning how to sail, taking turns cooking, and doing various other jobs around the boat. The number of dives offered will depend on weather and ice conditions.

Additionally, there are also private yachts for charter, usually taking a maximum of 12 passengers. This will probably be your most expensive option, but chartering a whole boat, particularly if with a group of divers, will give you more flexibility in your timings and choice of destinations.

For both of the sailing options, it is most important that you have a good skipper, experienced in Antarctic waters, so plan carefully and look for recommendation from others. The smaller and private yachts are often booked far in advance, and many are not available through traditional travel agents.

Choosing your vessel

The type of vessel you choose to travel on depends on your time constraints, budget, personal preferences, and destination. Prices for expeditions to Antarctica are variable between companies and ships. Divers have the choice of only a few of these companies, but the price is usually between $8,000–$25,000 USD, excluding air fare to the embarkation port, and usually an additional fee for diving, which includes the use of tanks and weights.

Every expedition ship is different and offers varying amenities. Some ships are quite luxurious with spa facilities and fine cuisine, while others are more basic. Whatever type you choose there are a few important things to look for when evaluating a dive operator:

- First impressions matter. When first contacting the company, do they seem well organized and professional?
- Experience counts. Has the company been running dive operations for a number of years, or is it a new venture?
- What type of ship or yacht do they use? Has it visited Antarctica regularly in the past?
- How many Zodiacs do they have? It is best to have one for every 10–12 passengers.
- How many divers do they allow to be on the trip, and what is the ratio between divers and divemasters?
- Are the divemasters experienced in Antarctic waters?
- How many dives will be offered during a trip?
- What type of emergency protocols do they have?

For information on Antarctic Tour Operators, visit **iaato.org**. This site offers general information and links to many of the companies that offer diving in Antarctica. **expeditiontrips.com** is a specialist agency run by people who have worked in the polar regions. They offer excellent, unbiased information on the various companies that are running tourist and dive operations.

Getting to your Expedition Vessel

The vast majority of ships going to the Antarctic sail from the ports of Punta Arenas in Chile or Ushuaia in Argentina. To get to either of these cities it is necessary to fly to one of two major airports, Buenos Aires in Argentina or Santiago in Chile, and then take a domestic flight. Flights into these cities can be accessed from all over the globe daily. If you are starting your voyage from Stanley in the Falkland Islands, there are scheduled flights from Santiago on certain days of the week. In order to guarantee availability, you should make your reservations a couple of months in advance. For UK residents who plan on starting their journey in the Falklands, there is a flight that departs approximately six times a month from RAF Brize Norton, near Burford, in Oxfordshire, England. For further details contact the Travel Co-ordinator, Falkland Islands Government Office, London, Tel: +44 (0)207 222 2542.

Most expedition operators have an air department who will help you book your flights. Flight coordinators will often make block bookings on a flight ahead of time, as scheduled flights to the 'world's end' can be sold out far in advance. Be sure to check with your booking agent about air travel. A special perk offered by a handful of companies make the journey quite simple by offering charter flights to the embarkation port from Buenos Aires or Santiago.

Of course the option of making your own arrangements is always open, and although it may be the more expensive choice, it will give you greater flexibility for extended travel. Buenos Aires and Santiago are both beautiful cities full of culture and history, so you may want to think about breaking your journey on the way to or from Antarctica to enjoy these cities.

If your journey originates outside the United States of America, you may wish to avoid flights through the United States. The USA does not offer 'in transit' facilities and you will have to go through immigration and customs formalities, regardless of final destination, which can be a lengthy procedure. Luggage restrictions are a real concern for divers. If your dive operator does not offer the ability to rent some of the heavier gear, such as regulators and dry suits, be sure to pack carefully. A helpful tip: taking an extra bag is often less expensive than an overweight bag.

All travelers will need a valid passport for their journey and, depending on your citizenship, you may need to make arrangements for a visa ahead of time. There can also be unexpected fees. For instance, all US, Canadian and Australian citizens will have to pay a reciprocity fee of approximately $160 USD in Buenos Aires. Citizens of the United States no longer need to pay a reciprocity fee in Santiago, Chile.

A great reference for all aspects of travel to Antarctica and these South American cities is the *Lonely Planet Guide to Antarctica*.

Ushuaia, Argentina

Requirements

Most of the operators taking divers to Antarctica expect at the **very least** a PADI Advanced Open Water, or equivalent, certification. Additionally, companies require a special Dry Suit Certification, and that you make at least 20 dry suit dives before boarding the ship. The divemasters will expect proof, not just your word, so be sure to bring a log book signed off by an instructor or divemaster. Wet suits are not an option in Antarctica.

Advanced Open Water and Dry Suit Diver Certifications are the **absolute minimum** that is asked for by dive operators. An additional requirement that some dive companies insist upon if an individual has not dived in the last six months, is that he or she must take a refresher course – and again proof will be needed. This refresher course allows the diver to practice their skills, and also provides a good opportunity to test out all of their equipment to make sure it works properly. Every company has their own policies, so be sure to check what is required for your expedition. Other certifications that may be asked for include Night Diving, Navigation, and Ice Diving

Medical evaluation

Many companies require their passengers to complete a medical waiver, signed by a doctor, stating that they are fit to travel. The form includes general information about medical history, medications, allergies, and any other problems. For those diving in Antarctica, an extra 'Diver Medical' is normally required.

The possibility of medical evacuation in a timely manner, or access to a hyperbaric chamber, is severely limited due to the lack of medical and transport facilities in Antarctica There are no hyperbaric chambers or shore-based medical facilities available to tourists, so should the need arise a casualty will have to go back to South America for treatment. It goes without saying that Antarctica is a long way from anywhere, and evacuation to a hospital or chamber would be a very lengthy process. Even in the best of circumstances a casualty would be at least 8 hours, and often well over 48 hours, away from a proper hospital. Some dive operators have a doctor specializing in diving medicine on their staff. Although this can be an advantage in the event of an injury, all a doctor can do is provide preliminary treatment.

SPECIAL NOTE

Diving in Antarctica is not something to be taken lightly, as it is one of the most extreme diving environments on the planet. Although you are traveling on a very comfortable diving platform, remember that you are far from immediate advanced medical facilities. As there are no hyperbaric chambers in Antarctica for tourist divers, most companies limit diving to profiles where decompression problems will not be an issue. Typically, this means a maximum depth of 18 m. Even so, divers need to be completely competent and safe in their diving techniques, and well trained in the use of the specialized equipment required. Make sure that when you leave to dive in Antarctica, you have not just come from a Caribbean holiday where you had the option to train in a dry suit for a few days. The more experience the better! Remember that even a veteran cold water diver can find Antarctica a challenge.

It is important that all who come to Antarctica, especially divers, are aware of the risks, and provide accurate medical information.

Medical and travel insurance

Medical evacuation from Antarctica can be very expensive, costing as much as $100,000 USD. Because of this, proper medical and travel insurance are recommended by all travel companies. It might be tempting to save money by skipping this additional expense, but keep in mind that you are traveling 500 miles from 'the end of the earth' (the common nickname of Tierra del Fuego).

There are a lot of travel insurance companies and policies, some which cover only trip refunds, and others that cover medical evacuations. I would suggest making sure that **worldwide** medical evacuation with no exclusions is covered in your policy. At the very least, read or request the information your travel company has to offer on this subject, allowing you to make an educated decision.

Many insurance policies exclude dangerous sports such as climbing and diving, so be sure to investigate. Divers may require additional insurance. The most common provider of this is DAN, which is recognized worldwide. DAN is a facilitator and insurer, but does not provide medical care for diving accidents. However, it does provide advice on initial treatment, evacuation, and hyperbaric treatment of dive-related injuries. If a diving accident occurs, DAN should be contacted immediately. DAN membership is relatively inexpensive and their insurance covers medical air evacuation from anywhere in the world for any injury or illness, not just for diving accidents. For an additional fee, divers can get secondary insurance coverage for decompression illness. DAN Americas can be reached at **diveralertnetwork.org**. European residents should contact **daneurope.org**.

Equipment

As in all diving, your equipment is what is keeping you alive while you breathe in a foreign environment. The harsh diving conditions of the Antarctic make high-quality and well maintained equipment even more important, and some specialized gear is needed.

All dive travel companies supply tanks and weights. Depending on how often you use cold-water gear will help you to make the decision as to whether to hire or buy equipment. However, some operators do offer equipment to hire. If gear is hired at home, you should do this early enough so that you can try out the equipment before you leave. If your local dive shop does not rent specialized gear, chances are they will know where to go.

In Antarctica it is advisable to have a back up, so doubling up on equipment as much as possible is a good idea. If something goes wrong with your gear, running to the local dive store is not an option, and a simple problem could ruin your trip.

The following is a list of the minimal dive gear you should bring on your expedition (your operator will provide a more comprehensive list):

- 2 sets of thermal underwear and/or Wooly Bear
- Dry suit
- Buoyancy Control Device (BCD) with low-pressure inflator
- Hood

- 2 pairs of dry gloves or exterior neoprene gloves
- 2 pairs of liner gloves
- 2 masks
- Quick release weight belt or weight retaining system with release buckles
- Clothing for cold protection at the surface. Sunglasses and hat, wind-proof outer jacket and pants
- 2 separate environmentally sealed or freeze protected regulator sets, as you will most likely be using special tanks with two separate outlets (H- or Y-Valves) *Check with the dive operator as to the type of tank valve that is used.
- 2 submersible pressure gauges
- Depth gauge, watch, and compass
- Knife
- Snorkel
- Fins
- Whistle
- Artificial spit (Defogging solution)
- Dive tables

Other equipment to take:
- Safety sausage with reel
- Dive light
- Dive computer
- Snorkel
- Compass
- Dive slate
- Camera and strobe
- Tank light
- Save-A-Dive kit
- Moldable mouthpieces for regulators

SPECIAL NOTES

1 Remember that regulators, dry suits, and Buoyancy Control Devices (BCDs) should be serviced annually, whether they have been used or not.

2 It is important to remember that batteries go flat more quickly in cold water than they do in warmer conditions. If you are using a computer and you can change the batteries personally, you should do so before the trip, bringing an extra battery just in case. If the computer has to be sent into the manufacturer for a battery change, you should send it in for service before you leave for your trip.

3 Although SCUBA is becoming more popular in Tierra del Fuego, there is no guaranteed place to rent equipment except if the operator is already set up to do so. Owning and knowing your own gear is preferable, but if you do choose to rent your equipment, you should either go to your local dive shop at home for assistance, or ask the company you are traveling with to recommend a supplier of rental equipment. You should make a few dives to get familiar with your gear before departing.

Under layers

Keep in mind that unless you have been diving in frozen lakes or quarries, the water in Antarctica will be between 4° and 15°C colder than you are used to, and you will feel every degree. It is a personal preference as to how many layers are donned below your dry suit but the following suggestions are based on my own experience.

The layer of clothing in contact with the skin should be one that 'wicks' away any moisture. The water and air temperature may be freezing, but you can certainly work up a sweat while gearing up, and it is important this moisture is transported away from your skin. On top of this wicking layer, several other layers can be donned for added warmth.

Personally, I have found it best to wear a base layer of polypropylene thermal underwear, and then a layer of expedition weight long-underwear. On top of this goes my fleece 'Wooly Bear' suit. And don't forget your socks! You may even need two pairs depending on how cold your toes get, but be sure to leave room for air and blood to circulate around your feet.

Dry suit

Everyone has a personal preference as to the type of dry suit they feel most comfortable in. There are a range of choices, ranging from crushed neoprene to tri-laminate.

The hands are almost always the first body part to get cold when diving in Antarctica, gradually becoming less dexterous as dive time increases. Usually it is the hands that ultimately decide the dive time, so it is important not to cut corners here.

Gloves come in a variety of styles from three fingered neoprene gloves, to integrated dry gloves. Whatever your choice, make sure you have adequate dexterity to get yourself out of sticky situations, making sure you can work the exhaust valves of your dry suit as well as your tank valves.

If you have room under your gloves, especially with integrated dry gloves, an extra pair of silk liners (or equivalent) is a good idea, and even chemical handwarmers if you are so inclined.

I also bring a pair of waterproof ski gloves to wear while gearing up, as already having cold fingers when entering the water can shorten dive time. A thick hood also helps to regulate the loss of heat, the benefits of which will be felt all over the body.

Full face mask vs. standard mask

A full face mask, as the name suggests, covers the whole face from forehead to chin. A regulator mouthpiece is built into the mask, which is attached by a low-pressure hose to the first stage of your regulator – essentially a second stage and mask all in one.

The full face mask has several advantages over a standard mask. It offers a slightly higher degree of warmth for the face, cutting down on the shock of entering the cold water. It can also allow communication with dive companions and the surface using the 'Buddy Phone.' Nevertheless, this mask is attached directly to the air supply, so if the regulator free-flows, or buddy breathing is needed, you must remove the mask and switch to a standard face mask.

Before jumping into the Antarctic water with a full face mask you should be properly trained in using this piece of equipment, especially in self-rescue, should something go wrong.

The standard face mask is the most comfortable and familiar to divers. Those diving in Antarctica tend to find the initial shock of having their skin exposed to the water quite jarring, even creating an 'ice-cream headache'. Thankfully, this diminishes within a few minutes as the body acclimates.

Most dive companies suggest using the standard face mask, as opposed to a full face mask. However, if you choose to bring a full face mask, you must also carry a standard mask on the dive in case your regulator free-flows or the full face mask floods.

Regulators

A diver in Antarctica should have environmentally sealed or freeze-protected regulators, but even these may freeze or free-flow at times. A free-flowing regulator is the most common technical difficulty a diver is likely to face in Antarctica.

Assuming the worst, that a regulator free-flows, it is recommended that everyone have a semi or fully redundant alternate air system. This means that you have two totally separate regulator set-ups, positioned on H- or Y-Valves, or on dual tanks. If something goes wrong and one of the regulators free-flows, the diver or buddy should be able to shut off the air supply to that regulator and make a comfortable switch to the back-up regulator. A switch of your low-pressure hose from the BCD to the dry suit may be needed as well, before ascent is made. The reason for this is if an air valve is shut off and the other regulator does not have dual low-pressure hoses, then a diver will need to take the low-pressure hose from his or her BCD in order to inflate the dry suit. A truly redundant system would be found on a dual tank set-up with all gauges and hoses doubled up.

If a diver is working on the Y-Valve system and cannot shut off the supply of air, a switch of second stages is needed to keep breathing comfortably. An Antarctic diver should know how to breathe through a free-flowing regulator, and this will be part of the required 'check-out' dive at the beginning of most trips. In the event of a free-flow, the dive should be aborted immediately, and a normal ascent made with a buddy, including safety stops if possible. *Do not* continue to dive with a free-flowing regulator, even if it is shut off; you have already used up your safety margin. Almost all manufacturers make an environmentally sealed, or freeze-protected regulator. Check with your local dive shop for the model that suits you best.

Leopard Stick

With the incidence of Leopard Seal sightings and harassment while diving increasing, some operators and many of the scientific bases have developed a Leopard Seal defense pole. This can be any kind of pole, PVC, metal, or aluminum, which at least one person in the buddy team carries, to fend off inquisitive Leopard Seal. (*See page 32: Leopard Seals – A diver's perspective*).

What to bring for your off time

Many divers will be on ships that integrate shore landings with diving, and even if aboard a small yacht where diving is the main activity you should still be prepared for landings and Zodiac excursions. The suggested list of clothing below, compiled from the packing lists of several expedition companies, will make you more comfortable and your trip more enjoyable.

- A bathing suit – some ships have saunas and some people take a 'polar plunge'.
- A good pair of binoculars.
- 2 or 3 pairs of warm, casual trousers to wear underneath your waterproof pants; polypropylene, wool, and/or corduroy are recommended. If you have ski pants, you might also include them in your selection of casual trousers.

- Electrical converter and adapter for use in your hotel during your journey to South America and on the vessel (most ships work on 220v European style (two round prongs), but you may get the occasional 110v North American plug (two flat prongs). Yachts use different systems.
- Cotton slacks (khakis, jeans, corduroy).
- Extra memory cards/film and batteries.
- 1 or 2 pairs waterproof ski mittens or gloves. You might bring a pair of thin, polypropylene gloves that fit under your ski mittens so that you can take your mittens off for photography without getting your hands cold. You may also want to bring an extra pair of mittens in case the other pair gets wet.
- T-shirts and other casual warm weather clothes, for layering and on board the ship.
- 2 or 3 warm woolen or polar fleece sweaters (a combination of lighter and heavier sweaters is preferable for greater flexibility). Please note that fleece is lighter and dries more quickly than wool.
- Calf-high waterproof boots with a strong non-skid sole (or traditional English Wellington rubber boots). Most landings will be wet (*i.e.* by Zodiac onto a beach). If you find walking in rubber boots difficult, then a good pair of water repellent hiking boots can be brought along. Landings may require using rubber boots, but once ashore, you can change to the hiking boots and leave the rubber boots at the landing.
- 1 wool ski cap and a scarf if the cap cannot be pulled down to cover your neck.
- 1 or 2 pairs of sturdy sunglasses with UV protection. The brightness of the summer sun reflected off the ice can be dangerous to under protected eyes. I recommend bringing a spare pair in case one breaks or is lost.
- Sunscreen and sunburn relief products.
- 1 full set of thermal or silk long underwear.
- Personal toiletries, including sun block, moisturizing lotion and lip balm to protect your skin from the harsh elements.
- Comfortable walking shoes with rubber soles (for onboard ship and sightseeing excursions), and walking sticks for uneven terrain.
- Water-resistant nylon backpack for carrying cameras or other equipment.
- 1 pair of waterproof pants (made of Gore-Tex or similar waterproof, breathable fabric) that are loose enough to wear over a regular pair of trousers. You will need these for almost every landing.
- Antarctic Parka – waterproof, windproof, hooded, and down or fleece lined. This is quite often supplied through the travel company.
- 1 waterproof rain jacket for rainy or windy weather that is too warm for a parka.
- 3 or 4 pairs of warm, sturdy, long wool socks and an equal number of thin socks to wear underneath for extra insulation.
- Zip-lock plastic bags as added protection for camera, memory cards/film, *etc.*

SPECIAL NOTE

Many divers dream about diving under the Antarctic ice. Although some of the diving that is done from expedition ships may take place under small areas of ice, it is unlike the pictures you may have seen of divers entering the water through a hole in three-meter-thick fast ice. Any ice diving you may experience will be in a controlled environment under small floes, with easily accessed exit points.

Body responses

Diving in Antarctica's freezing water is a physiological stress on the body. Remember when you jumped into a cold lake early in the summer? The reaction you had is the same that many divers face in Antarctica. Initial shortness of breath and a pounding heart is caused by various body systems trying to react to the overload of impulses from the nerves, telling the brain "It's freezing! Please compensate!" This usually lasts only a minute or so, diminishing with experience, but as a rule of thumb if you are really uncomfortable it is wise to not continue with the dive.

Once fully immersed, a diver may experience discomfort as the face becomes numb. This process usually lasts about 2 minutes, after which a diver generally cannot feel the parts of the face exposed to the water. Not able to feel their lips, divers grip their regulator hard with their teeth to make sure it is securely in the mouth, which can lead to one or two problems over time: mouthpieces tend to be bitten through more often; and with sustained diving in freezing waters, a diver may actually end up grinding down his or her teeth.

Thankfully, a moldable mouthpiece has come onto the market, which fits the mouth and teeth like a mouth guard, cutting down on teeth grinding and making it easier to keep your 2nd stage in place.

Despite being dressed as warmly as possible, the longer the bottom time in Antarctica, the colder a diver is going to get. As body temperature drops, even slightly, the body tries to compensate – the first response is shivering. Shivering is a healthy reaction to cold, as the muscle movement caused by shivering creates energy and friction (*i.e.* heat). For divers, shivering is not a huge crisis, but is a constant reminder of how cold one is, which can spoil a dive.

Frostbite is a real possibility while diving in Antarctica, especially in body areas that are fully exposed to the water. Once affected, not only can frostbite inhibit you from diving during the rest of the trip, but it is also a prolonged and commonly reoccurring problem, as the area of frostbite becomes hypersensitive and more prone to frostbite in the future.

One way to stave off frostbite is to use a very thick lotion (Vaseline also works well) on the face and hands. This puts an added layer between the skin and direct contact with the water.

Conditions

Conditions and bathymetry at each site differ greatly, and may further vary according to weather and time of the season. Each site is affected by ice, wind, current, and surge in a different way, and this may change weekly or even daily. However, the type of dive – wall, slope – do not change, and these features are described in *The Dive Sites* section of this book; quick reference icons are also included for each site.

Mode of Transportation

Unless you are traveling on a boat fitted with a dive platform, divers in Antarctica are typically taken to the dive site by Zodiac. These inflatable boats, of which Zodiac is one brand, come in a variety of sizes and may be semi- or fully inflatable. They are the mainstay of transportation for all visitors to Antarctica, and the perfect means of getting to the dive sites, as well as a ready surface support boat. Zodiacs are easy to get in and out of, and most boat crews are very helpful to the diver while gearing up, entering, and exiting the water.

Almost all expedition vessels store their Zodiacs on deck, hauling them up and down the side of the ship or boat by crane. The diving equipment, including tank and BCD set-up, weights, and fins, is usually placed inside the Zodiac and lowered to the water, or passed down from a lower deck to the Zodiac. Divers board the Zodiac down a ladder, gangway, or through a tender-entrance in the ship's side.

Visibility

You may have seen pictures from McMurdo Sound in the Ross Sea where the visibility can sometimes exceed 100 m. These conditions occur under the fast ice in the winter or early spring, before the light levels increase and the ice breaks up, triggering plankton blooms. These are not the conditions divers will encounter in high summer around the Antarctic Peninsula or South Georgia.

Being further north, the ice around the peninsula breaks up earlier in the season, releasing plankton from under the ice, and dispersing it throughout the water. As the water warms throughout the season, the plankton population can grow exponentially, turning the water green and decreasing visibility.

The water around the peninsula has a cycle of good and bad visibility. In general the initial plankton bloom is in early to mid-December; the water becomes extremely green, and visibility can drop to less than a meter. Visibility changes from dive site to dive site through the season, sometimes clearing for a short period of time before deteriorating again. Generally by the end of January or early February the water begins to clear for the winter. A visit either very early or late in the season will allow for the best clear water photography.

Depth

In the description of each dive site, the maximum depth that the site allows is indicated. For instance 'The Shag Wall' at Paradise Harbor (*page 88*) would allow a recreational dive to 40 meters, although this is not recommended. Except on rare occasions, most operators and divemasters limit dives to 22 m.

Time

Dive times are likely to be shorter than you are used to. Depending on a diver's tolerance for cold, the dive may last between 15 and 45 minutes, the average being 30 minutes.

Water temperature

Salt water has a much lower freezing point than fresh water. This allows the sea water to stay in liquid form at temperatures where fresh water would be solid. The actual freezing point of sea water depends on salinity and depth, but averages −1·8°C at the surface. Water temperature on the peninsula does not vary much during the year, remaining between −1·8° and 1°C.

What you might see

When compared to other aquatic environments, such as the Giant Kelp forest, Antarctica's

benthos are quite small. It takes an enormous expenditure of energy for an animal to grow in the frigid waters of Antarctica, a place where staying alive and relatively warm is the most important goal, and growth is considered secondary.

For this reason, the creatures a diver comes across are usually undersized, so take the time to look for the small things, like nudibranchs, amphipods, and worms that abound here.

You may have the rare opportunity to dive or snorkel with a seal, so take care and follow the *Marine Wildlife Watching Guidelines* that are set for all Antarctic visitors (see *page 126*).

The underwater world of Antarctica can be a weird and wonderful place. It is filled with creatures that look similar to those in your nightmares and dreams – giant bugs and graceful seals. I am always amazed at the resilience and diversity of the benthos, as well as the brilliant colors that line the nooks and crannies – rays of sunshine in what some would call a cold, dark, and unforgiving world. If there is any advice I can give, it is to take the time to appreciate what you are seeing in a place on the planet where very few divers have ever ventured.

LEOPARD SEALS – A SCIENTIFIC PERSPECTIVE

Shona Muir – British Antarctic Survey (BAS)

As one of the top predators in the Antarctic, Leopard Seals (*Hydrurga leptonyx*) present a risk to humans Scuba diving (hereafter referred to simply as diving) and snorkeling in the Antarctic region. There is a lack of detailed information on the nature of interactions divers and snorkelers have with Leopard Seals. However as a direct result of the death of a snorkeler in Antarctica in July 2003, efforts have recently been made to attempt to quantify the likelihood of interactions and to provide information to enable more appropriate assessment of the hazards and risk associated with Leopard Seals.

Human perceptions of Leopard Seals, as with any large, predatory species, have been inevitably shaped by historical accounts of interactions with humans that have occurred since the *Heroic Age* of Antarctic exploration in the early Twentieth Century. Several historic accounts of interactions have been published, as well as more contemporary anecdotal accounts, which have portrayed Leopard Seals as 'evil', 'feared creatures', 'beasts', resembling 'small dinosaurs' with a 'sinister reputation'. Lansing's 1959 account of Leopard Seal encounters in 1916 in *Endurance, Shackleton's Incredible Voyage* is one such portrayal. This section draws on accounts with a more balanced perspective that have attempted to provide more appropriate assessment of the risks Leopard Seals present to divers and snorkelers, based on a range of interactions from a fatal attack from a Leopard Seal to interactions where physical contact did not occur.

Leopard seal biology and behaviour

Leopard seals are distributed within the circumpolar pack ice surrounding the Antarctic continent and their population is estimated to be 222,000 to 440,000. In addition to the normal distribution in relation to the Antarctic pack ice, they disperse northwards to subantarctic islands such as South Georgia and Macquarie Island during the winter. In general these extra-limital records involve juveniles that appear to move further north during the winter. Leopard seals have also been recorded in Chile, Argentina, the Falkland Islands, South Africa, New Zealand and Australia. The most northerly recordings of Leopard Seals have been from the Cook Islands.

The Leopard Seal is the largest of the four species of seal that breed in the high Antarctic, the others being Weddell *Leptonychotes weddellii*, Crabeater *Lobodon carcinophagus* and Ross Seals *Ommatophoca rossii*. Its scientific name, *Hydrurga leptonyx*, translates from the Greek as the 'slender-clawed worker in the water'. Females (up to 3·8 m in length and 500 kg in weight) are generally larger than males (3·3 m and 300 kg).

However, anecdotal sightings of Leopard Seals have indicated that they may attain lengths in excess of 4 m. They generally have a silver/grey pelage which is darker dorsally, often spotted with dark grey and black spots. The Leopard Seal has a distinct reptilian profile with a long and slender body, a large 'shoulder' and a disproportionately large head with a long snout. They have powerful jaws and large re-curved canines and incisors as well as upper and lower tricuspids molars that interlock.

Leopard seals are generally solitary and are catholic feeders. Their diet varies with season and location and includes penguins, seals, krill, fish, cephalopods and crustaceans. Although detailed behaviour varies greatly between individual Leopard Seals, distinct hunting techniques have been observed mainly in the water and at the ice edge. Most observations of hunting have been of Leopard Seals preying on penguins or seals either by ambush (wherein the seal lies at the surface, often with only its nostrils breaking the surface, in a place where prey are known to be abundant), by stalking under thin ice and breaking through the ice with their head to capture penguins, or by pursuit hunting where the seal makes no attempt to hide itself and relies of swimming speed to capture its prey.

A fatal attack by a Leopard Seal

On 22 July 2003, Kirsty Brown, a 28-year-old marine biologist with the British Antarctic Survey (BAS), was snorkeling with her partner (buddy) 20 meters from shore. They were studying iceberg scouring at South Cove and Ryder Bay, Rothera Research Station, Adelaide Islands (67°34' S, 68°07' W) on the Antarctic Peninsula. The conditions were calm and overcast (wind 2 kts from 80 degrees, cloud cover 7 octas and increasing). The air temperature was −8·1°C and the local sea-surface was covered by grease-ice (<1 cm thickness). Water visibility was recorded as good (>30 m). The two snorkelers had entered the water at 15:10 local time, whilst two personnel maintained a safety watch from ashore. A few minutes later, when both snorkelers were within 20 m of the shore and were approximately 15–20 m apart, Kirsty screamed and disappeared from view. As her snorkeling partner started to swim towards where Kirsty disappeared, the shore party saw Kirsty briefly resurface together with a Leopard Seal. The shore party immediately made a MAYDAY call to the research station operations room (at 15:25) and a rescue boat was launched. As the snorkeling partner reached the point at which Kirsty was last seen he could see her submerged at 5 m with a Leopard Seal holding her fin. At this point the snorkeling buddy returned to join the shore party.

At 15:35 the seal resurfaced, approximately 1 km from where it had last been seen. It was holding Kirsty, who was face down in the water, by the head. As the rescue boat approached one

Sequence of photos showing a Leopard Seal taking an Emperor Penguin from the ice edge...

of the members of the boat party began hitting the water and the Leopard Seal with a shovel. The Leopard Seal released Kirsty and remained in the vicinity of the boat. Kirsty was then pulled into the boat and emergency first aid was administered. The boat immediately returned to shore where Kirsty was transferred to the Rothera Surgery under the direction of the base doctor. After full assessment and prolonged attempts at resuscitation, CPR was stopped and Kirsty was pronounced dead at 16:50 hours.

The Coroner's Inquest into Kirsty's death recorded a verdict of accidental death, caused by drowning due to a Leopard Seal attack. The Coroner paid tribute to Rothera personnel, and said that he had been very impressed by the professionalism and skill of everyone involved, in particular those directly involved in the incident. He stated that the tragedy was a reminder of the dangers encountered when conducting research in the Antarctic.

Kirsty was 156 cm tall and weighed 55 kg, and she was wearing a black dry suit and black fins. Her dive computer, which had been reset prior to entering the water, recorded a maximum depth of 70·1 m. The sex of the Leopard Seal was not determined. However, it was estimated to be 4·5 m in length, measured with reference to the rescue boat, indicates that it may have been an unusually large female.

In response to the death of Kirsty Brown, BAS temporarily suspended diving and snorkeling activities while a review of diving and snorkeling safety was undertaken. Diving re-commenced in January 2004, with a number of revisions to the diving procedures, although snorkeling is now prohibited. These revisions include a 30-minute period of observation of marine mammals prior to a diver entering the water, a boat party to accompany all dives and the use of diver to surface communications.

The nature of Leopard Seal interactions with divers and snorkelers

In an attempt to increase the level of knowledge of the nature (*i.e.* the location, activity and timing) of Leopard Seal interactions with divers and snorkelers, one study in 2004/05 measured the response of Leopard Seals to humans in different situations, using a categorical response scale. Location of the Leopard Seal and human had the greatest influence on the response of the Leopard Seal. More specifically, interactions occurring at the ice edge resulted in the highest response from Leopard Seals, where Leopard Seals seek out prey. This information is pertinent to divers or snorkelers who undertake under ice diving, entering the ice either through a dive hole, or who enter the water at the ice edge.

An examination of dive and snorkel logs indicated that interactions that occurred while the human was in the water generally described the seal's behaviour as displaying curiosity, and occurred most frequently at the surface. Curiosity is essential to the acquisition of

Sequence of photos showing a Leopard Seal taking an Emperor Penguin from the ice edge...

knowledge and is fundamental to ensure that individual animals are optimally adapted to their environment. Although Leopard Seals approached close to observers and displayed behaviour that appeared aggressive, there were no records of interactions where 'curious' Leopard Seals showed subsequent hunting, or attack, behaviour. There were no attacks where both the seal and the observer were in the water (apart from that on Kirsty Brown).

In contrast, in most interactions (only a few occasions) where physical contact was initiated by a seal, in the form of an attack, the seal was not seen prior to the attack. The majority of these limited occasions occurred at the edge of the ice. An explanation for such attacks by Leopard Seals at the ice-edge could be the mistaken identity of humans as prey or simply identification as prey. Given the numbers of penguins in the Antarctic compared to the very limited number (and distribution) of people it is hardly surprising that such mistakes occur. It is also noteworthy that penguins, the only thing other than humans that stand vertically at the ice-edge, are one of the most frequent prey of Leopard Seals. It has been suggested that once a seal realizes a mistake has been made, the attack would be likely to be discontinued. In this case we are fortunate to be lacking sufficient data to evaluate this suggestion.

The incident that resulted in the death of Kirsty Brown is the only known account of its kind, given that physical contact occurred at the surface of the water, and that the seal had not been seen prior to the event. The behaviour of the seal that killed Kirsty Brown (*i.e.* capture, followed by prolonged submersion and then a return to the surface at a location some distance from the initial submersion site), along with the bite marks on Kirsty's head, are consistent with the Leopard Seal hunting behaviour described above. The data from the dive computer that Kirsty was wearing is the first piece of information on the sub-surface behaviour of Leopard Seals during a feeding attack. The rapid descent to 70 m and ascent suggests that Leopard Seals may undertake rapid, deep dives whilst holding large prey items before returning to the surface some point remote from the point of initial capture.

The likelihood of interactions with Leopard Seals

An assessment of the likelihood of interactions with Leopard Seals should be based on a knowledge of when such interactions have taken place previously, the geographical location, and the planned activity. Studies have indicated that there is a very strong spatio-temporal pattern in the periods when Leopard Seals are present at Antarctic localities. Data from the 2004/05 study showed very different patterns of abundance at Bird Island, South Georgia (July to September), Signy Island, South Orkney (October to January, and in May) and Rothera, Antarctic Peninsula (December to January). Such a distribution pattern reflects the seasonal advance and retreat of the pack ice, the preferred habitat of Leopard Seals.

In addition to the seasonal movements of Leopard Seals, the human population of Antarctic regions is also highly seasonal, with numbers in summer far exceeding those in winter. As technology and logistic support makes human travel and presence in Antarctica easier, that presence is increasing and inevitably humans are likely to encounter Leopard Seals more frequently. The potential for such encounters is highest in the vicinity of research stations and along popular tourist destinations, particularly along the Antarctic Peninsula.

A detailed analysis of BAS dive records suggests that the number of sightings of, and interactions with, marine mammals was simply a function of the total number of dives and there was no evidence of a change in frequency of interactions over time. Detailed dive log data indicated that sightings and interactions with Leopard Seals have most frequently occurred at or near the surface. On the basis of >30 years of BAS dive data there is a likelihood of interacting with a Leopard Seal on approximately 1 in every 200 dives, and the likelihood of sustaining a physical injury from a Leopard Seal is of the order of 1 in 9,000 dives.

Possible influences on the risk of interactions

The consequences of sustaining injuries caused by a Leopard Seal may be amplified by the typically extreme conditions of the Antarctic. Leopard seal hunting and predatory behaviour, described in relation to the nature of the interactions, possible precursors to attack, and human behaviour should be taken into consideration to potentially reduce the risk to humans involved in encounters with Leopard Seals.

Research has investigated whether there was any evidence of seal behaviors that may act as precursors to higher level of aggression during interactions with humans. Despite personnel that have worked extensively with Leopard Seals in captivity, on ice and on land, suggesting a range of behaviours that may precede more aggressive behaviour, no conclusive evidence has been obtained. Such behaviours include sudden head movements or jabs, extensions of the neck, vocalizations including a snort in and a blast out of air, and intentionally making eye contact. Precursors to heightened behaviour in water may be circling-in towards the person in the water, approaching towards the head, and blowing air or bubbles. However, the perception of aggression by an observer may not actually reflect an increase in aggression from the seal.

Similarly, there appears to be no conclusive evidence that specific human behaviours may result in an increased response from a Leopard Seal, although a number have been suggested; these include blowing bubbles, trapping/blocking the seal's exit, moving rapidly, and turning away. Suggestions of human behaviours that may reduce the likelihood of a

Sequence of photos showing a Leopard Seal taking an Emperor Penguin from the ice edge.

response from a Leopard Seal have also been made, including doing nothing but facing the animal and retreating slowly if the interaction escalates. It is, however, important to be constantly vigilant, as awareness of a Leopard Seal's presence is crucial to reacting without panicking.

The majority of interactions between divers and snorkelers and Leopard Seals in the water appear to be just the seal's inquisitiveness. The fatal attack of Kirsty Brown is the only known incident of its kind, given that physical contact occurred at the surface of the water, and that the seal had not been seen prior to the event. Nonetheless, this fatal accident indicates that Leopard Seals can display predatory behaviour towards humans and that the associated risks should be recognized.

LEOPARD SEALS – A DIVER'S PERSPECTIVE

Göran Ehlmé – Founder Waterproof Dive Equipment and co-founder of Waterproof Expeditions

I have been working with Leopard Seals for many years, returning to Antarctica each austral summer to dive with or film these incredible animals. Over the past few years, the Leopard Seal has risen from relative obscurity, to being one of the most recognized animals in the world, thanks to publications such as *National Geographic* and movies such as *Happy Feet*. Equally, this publicity has created a certain aura around the animal, and despite very little research being done on the species, it has become one of the most feared and coveted animals in Antarctica. Through my experiences, I have developed a kind of love affair with the Leopard Seal, and would like to share some of my trysts. I hope that by reading my personal anecdotes, you too will begin to see what an impressive creature the Leopard Seal really is.

But before I continue, first and foremost it is important to remember that the Leopard Seal is a wild animal. They are governed by the rules of survival in one of the most inhospitable environments in the world, and not bound by the congenial behaviors of man. No one should ever take being with a wild animal for granted. Like any other creature, the Leopard Seal has unpredictable behaviors. For instance, just moments after you enter the water, a Leopard Seal may swim straight at you, opening its jaws. All instincts tell us that this is an aggressive behavior, creating a sense of fear and shock in ourselves. Fortunately, despite the immediate feeling of being attacked, this is usually not the case. However, it does take a certain amount of time with the Leopard Seal to understand their body language; look at its movements – does it swim with an impression of grace and calmness, or is it bellowing and making jerky motions? Just like sea lions, Leopard Seals are intelligent and curious animals who crave interaction, but perhaps if a sea lion had a mouth of teeth like that, we wouldn't think they were so cute. Each seal is different, and the key is to stay sharp while you are in their presence, still allowing yourself to enjoy their grace and power, yet aware of strange or skittish behaviors.

The first divers to encounter a 'Lep' face-to-face were Doug Allan and Peter Scones, while shooting a sequence for *Life in the Freezer*. For those of us who have seen the production, it is an unforgettable progression of events as the Leopard Seal is at first simply swimming in the frame, and by the end presenting a penguin to Doug. You can almost feel the anticipation as this 12 foot female swims up and pushes (albeit gently) the penguin to the camera.

Just before the first time I got in the water with Leopard Seals, I asked Doug if he thought I would have any problems. He said he didn't think so, but take a ski pole just in case. Within the first minute of entering the water I had a HUGE female open her jaws and place her jagged teeth just centimeters from my face. I must admit I was extremely uncomfortable and took off like a shot out of the water. Many years and many seals have passed since that day, and I now find myself feeling an immense sense of peace and happiness while diving with Leopard Seals.

Several years ago there was a tragic loss of life caused by a Leopard Seal – the only death on record – which sent shock waves through the entire Antarctic community, from national programs to tourist organizations. A lot of thought and investigation has gone into this attack, and new safety policies have been created in order to avoid senseless accidents such as this in the future. I have thought quite a bit to myself as to why this happened. Why would an intelligent animal such as the Leopard Seal attack a human, something that it has never done before? In doing so it took a huge risk unto itself, as the seal would have no idea how strong a human is and what kind of harms way it was putting itself into. My only conclusion is that this was an animal which, cut off from its food source by the pack ice, was starving, and any starving animal can be a dangerous animal.

While filming BBC's *Blue Planet*, Martha Holmes, Doug Allan, and I were in the Ross Sea, attempting to gather Emperor Penguin footage. We would sit at the pack ice edge where the Emperor Penguins came and went from the colony. Hundreds of birds would gather there, until one, and then another, and then the rest would hurl themselves into the sea, right over the hidden, yet awaiting jaws of the Leopard Seal. The Leopard Seal's tactic is to sit just under the ice edge, concealed and waiting. Its senses are triggered by the sound of crunching ice or footsteps above, at which point is ready to charge at full power grabbing whatever is on the ice edge. It is in hunting ecstasy, a bit like the Great White Shark's feeding frenzy, so the seal cannot always distinguish what is really an Emperor Penguin or what isn't. For the first few days, our film crew was charged several times, which of course can be quite dangerous because once caught you could be dragged under the ice. However, the Leopard Seals did learn to distinguish our footsteps and shadows, but just the same, when approaching a new ice edge, always be wary until given the all clear by your guide.

Most of my encounters have happened during the summer months of Antarctica, when the sea is ripe with krill and the penguin colonies are full of birds, creating an abundance of food for the Leopard Seal. Each seal I have dived with has had a separate personality, some are shy, some are gentle, some are tough, and some are sweet. One summer I had a 'private' seal I named Yellowbelly. She was a large animal that loved to keep me company while I was filming other seals. She would often tickle my neck with her whiskers (as you might imagine this was a little disconcerting at first), and follow me down on dives, even to 20 or 30 m. While at the surface in my boat, she would actually sleep next to the hull, her ventilations echoing throughout the night. I am not sure when it was, but she started to kill penguins for me – 1, 2, 3, 4, or 5 a day – surrounding me with their poor carcasses, but thankfully she eventually lost interest and continued only being an observer. During our 'relationship' I never touched

her, and her only touch to me was with her whiskers; "Our love was beyond physical contact," I used to write to my girlfriend back home. Although I have had other seals trying to 'feed' me, I have never seen Yellowbelly again.

Over the years I have been very fortunate to have so many spectacular encounters with the Leopard Seal, and the knowledge I pass on to you is only from days and hours of hands-on experience. While there is still much speculation about the animal, I personally feel that the Leopard Seal is one of the most beautiful and fantastic animals in our oceans.

The Sea Leopard Project

To understand the behavior, ecology and population dynamics of Leopard Seals on the Antarctic Peninsula in order to promote their conservation and safe human-seal interactions.

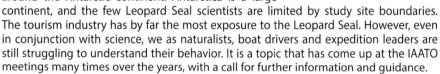

A true ice seal, the Leopard Seal is one of the least-studied pinnipeds in the world, with only a handful of scientists gathering information from around the Antarctic continent. Antarctica is a large continent, and the few Leopard Seal scientists are limited by study site boundaries. The tourism industry has by far the most exposure to the Leopard Seal. However, even in conjunction with science, we as naturalists, boat drivers and expedition leaders are still struggling to understand their behavior. It is a topic that has come up at the IAATO meetings many times over the years, with a call for further information and guidance.

The Sea Leopard Project (**www.sealeopardproject.org**) was founded in 2009 to gather data using tourism industry resources to further our understanding of the distribution, vocalizations, feeding habits and, most importantly, the interactions between humans and Leopard Seals.

Some interesting findings from the 2011 to 2013 summer seasons of data collection are:

- Based on its spot patterning and other scarring, the same Leopard Seal has been identified between Pleneau and Booth Islands, thus indicating territoriality.
- A Leopard Seal can be protective of 'its' piece of ice, no matter how small, and will return to it repeatedly. If a viewing boat gets between the seal and its favored piece of ice there is a chance of an aggressive interaction, usually in the form of a bitten pontoon, the risk increasing exponentially the closer the boat gets.

This is information that has been gleaned from just a few 'citizen science' contributors: imagine the data that could be collected if all the water-based travelers in Antarctica were to cooperate.

In addition to the tourism community, the Sea Leopard Project also collaborates with pinniped scientists from the United States, Great Britain, Argentina and Australia. Any information that is obtained is shared and used to gain a greater understanding of the Leopard Seal and its activities around the Antarctic continent.

UNDERWATER PHOTOGRAPHY AND VIDEOGRAPHY IN ANTARCTICA

Göran Ehlmé – 2006 BBC Shell Wildlife Photographer of the Year

After taking both still and video images in Antarctica for many years, there are some things I would like to share with you …

The waters surrounding Antarctica are some of the most incredible, yet difficult environments in the world in which to take video or photographs. Conditions of low light, high particulate matter and surge are often combined, creating a challenge for even the most experienced of underwater photographers. The common perception is that as Antarctic waters are so cold (between – 1·9°C – 0°C) they are absent of life. But nothing could be further from the truth. Antarctica has one of the richest marine environments in the world and is full of surprises. The creatures found there are colorful and astonishing, offering many opportunities for stunning and unique images.

Preparation

Earlier in this book is a section dedicated to the type of diving gear – cameras excluded – that you should consider bringing on your expedition. Here, I will do the same in relation to camera equipment but the principles of being as familiar with your kit as you can applies to everything from a properly sized dry suit, to the right kind of filter on your camera lens.

First, I must say that this section should not be taken as an introduction of how to shoot underwater in Antarctica or elsewhere. You should not spend your precious time in Antarctica learning, you should be comfortable and proficient with your gear before you start your journey south. It is a common theme nowadays, especially with a busy work life, that we do not take the time to prepare as well as we would like for our 'vacations.' However, for many, a trip to the Antarctic is a once and a lifetime vacation, and one which should not be looked upon lightly. While you are in Antarctica, whether you are on land or under the sea, you want everything to go as smoothly as possible, so you can enjoy it that much more.

Often we treat ourselves to new gear before big expeditions, assuming we will have enough time to learn and become comfortable with it once we get our trip underway. Unfortunately, we grossly underestimate the time available, and the complexity of our gear, making it is quite conceivable you may not even open your camera cases during the crossing of the Drake Passage. This may leave only a few hours before your first dive to familiarize yourself, so it is important to learn your equipment, all of your equipment from regulators to cameras, before you leave home.

If you are not familiar with underwater shooting, I suggest you get a good beginners book or take an introductory class so that you know the basics before you start your expedition. Getting to know your equipment and shooting with it is the most important thing, even if you can only spend time in a pool photographing tiles to do so. This practice will not only allow you to get used to your dry suit and other essential dive equipment, but will also give you the building blocks needed to maximize your time underwater: you want the operation of your equipment to be almost second nature. Write down your favorite camera settings on a plastic write card, and analyze your images, making notes of what works best in which situation. The first thing that will begin to get uncomfortable during a dive, no matter what kind of gloves you wear, will be your hands. Although you may not be able to simulate the cold, get used to switching the small knobs and buttons on the underwater housing with large cumbersome gloves. You should be able to find your shutter release without having to look for it, you should know exactly where to go in the menu to change the speed of your camera, and all of this should be done relatively quickly (as quickly as you can move with 35 kg of gear on your back). In all aspects, Antarctica is unpredictable, so you may have your camera set for shooting benthic animals, when a Leopard Seal appears. You'll have to move fast in order to capture the image.

Equipment

Since I started photographing underwater, I have had the great fortune to experience a revolution in the way images are taken. It took decades for cameras and the quality of equipment to change, but the advent of digital and HD has taken underwater photography and videography to a new level. Instead of being confined to 36 frames a dive, where the mix of natural light, strobes, and particles in the water often made it difficult to predict outcomes, we now have options upon options. Today, we can see the results immediately and make adjustments accordingly – and have instant gratification! We can take hundreds of pictures or hours of footage on each dive, and although only one may give us the image we want, at least the option is open to us. Better still, cameras continue to improve and give us enhanced quality all the time.

Anemone *Isotella antarctica*

Digital photography has opened the door for the holiday photographer, those of us who really only get the chance to take underwater pictures when we are on vacation. We may not have the largest or most sophisticated cameras and/or housing, but enjoy photographing subjects underwater. Don't let those small 'point-and-shoot' cameras fool you, some have amazing features, and allow a lot of freedom.

Yet with advanced technology come additional things to worry about. Electronics do not like water or moisture, so it is important to take the following into account: once your camera has been set up and exposed to the cold outside, NEVER bring it inside the ship or cabin, or any other place that is warm. If you bring your camera into a warm area, and then open it up, the moisture in the air will condense onto the camera that will then become wet. Antarctica may be the driest place on earth, but you can bet your camera will find any moisture there is in the air. Likewise, if you open up the digital card compartment, it will also attract the moisture, and may not only ruin your card but the pictures that are on it as well. Your best bet is to leave your camera, in the housing, outside for a while, so that it drips off, and later dry it with a towel. Then take it to a sheltered place, still in a cold environment, remove the card and the battery and place them in a Zip-lock bag, and allow them to warm up for an hour or two before opening the bag again. If possible, it is best to keep the camera and housing outside (sheltered of course), which means you only have to worry about changing the card and the battery. In polar regions, the rule of thumb is that battery power will be half of what it is normally – so if your batteries are old buy new ones before you leave, and always bring spares.

Another trade secret is to bring lots of silica gel bags (the kind found in shoe boxes) to soak up moisture – place them in your housing and change them frequently. For those who

Dragon Fish *Chaenocephalus aceratus*

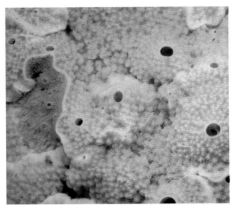

Unidentified sponge

Tunicate *Cnemidocarpa verrucosa* and
Brittle star *Ophionotus victoriae*

are only 'terrestrial' photographers, this advice applies to your 'topside' cameras as well; at the very least make sure you bring a waterproof bag to protect them when in boats or bad weather.

Regardless of your precautions, sometimes a little patch of moisture forms at the center of the lens, especially with lenses that actually have contact with the water. This usually disappears in 30–60 minutes, just before you finish your dive. It is most often caused by direct sunlight heating up the lens of your camera, so whenever possible keep the camera covered and out of the elements (this also applies to your time in the Zodiac). Quite often during a season, I travel with my camera in a Coleman cooler, although this is slightly difficult in terms of the luggage allowance.

Purchasing a housing for your camera can be a mind-boggling experience as there are so many choices; some are made of aluminum, some are synthetic, some are negatively buoyant, and some are positive. If a suggestion can be made, it would be to make sure your camera and housing are slightly buoyant, but again this is a personal preference. Think of it as a safety precaution for yourself and your rig just in case it is dropped into the water. You would be surprised how many times your camera changes hands: it is handed down into the support boat, then to you in the water, you will carry it with you throughout the dive, then hand it back up after the dive into the support boat, and eventually back onto the ship. It only takes one person with cold or inflexible hands to drop it… Even with the best intentions of keeping it positively buoyant, the addition of external pieces such as strobes may make the rig negative, so a safety cord is another good precaution to take.

Shooting Techniques

The best days of shooting above the water come not when it is sunny with blue skies, but when it is a little overcast. This also applies to underwater photography as no camera likes large variations in light. Antarctic waters have a lot of particulate matter in them, even when they appear to be clear. It is the sign of a healthy ocean, but can wreak havoc with your exposures, and create 'backscatter'. Some of the problems that might arise are as follows:

1) We all dream of shooting the intricate patterns found in ice, but these magnificent ice structures can break the light beams, and cause 'bad' reflections that get overexposed.

2) Almost all the picture-worthy animals in Antarctica, from penguins to nudibranchs, have some white on their body, yet are immersed in an external environment that can be extremely dark, again affecting the exposure.

3) Likewise, when you are in shallow water shooting penguins or seals, while trying to compensate for the light reflection from the surface and progressively darker water, whiter body parts can get over-exposed

Gastropod *Pellilitorina pellita*

To handle the above problems, make sure that you watch your exposure and adjust the F-stop accordingly. Additionally, if you have seals or penguins in natural light, make sure you have the camera set on a higher speed.

When shooting, always think as wide as possible, except when shooting macro. Forget your zoom, unless you have a wide-angle zoom, as it is always better to be as panned-out as possible, and then move closer to your subject (if you can). When a subject is moving, or your auto-focus is having a problem tracking, it can be helpful to use your fin as a focusing point and lock the camera at that distance. By doing this, and using a small aperture (high F-stop), objects that are anywhere from fairly close to the lens to infinity should be in sharp focus.

Nudibranch *Cuthona* sp.

Usually a lot of the 'diving' with penguins, seals, and whales is never done with a tank, but rather using a snorkel. When I worked with Paul Nicklen during his *National Geographic* Leopard Seal assignment, we almost always snorkeled. A snorkel gives you the advantage of being quick and silent, which is key to a good encounter. However, this type of photographic activity usually leads to your camera rising out of and falling into the water, especially if you are attempting half-and-half shots. The problem with this is that small air bubbles often collect on the front of the lens, even when wiped with Rain-X. Get into the habit of wiping your lens as often as you can. There is nothing so annoying as having a good image obscured by bubbles.

When snorkeling with all animals in Antarctica the ambient light is generally enough for pictures. However, even at shallow depths a strobe may give that added 'life's light' to the animal's eye.

Diver using video

Shooting animals

Crabeater Seals are usually in large groups. If you move slowly, you may pique their interest, causing them to come up to you, especially the younger seals which are a bit more curious.

Antarctic Fur Seals are curious and excellent to dive with. They will come in close to investigate, so make sure you have your camera set on a high speed, and the lens at as wide-angle as possible. However, there are times that 'furries' can get a bit too much, making physical contact with you and your gear, so it is possible you may have to abort the dive.

Weddell Seals are often found in shallow bays or hauled out close to shore. They are a shy seal if you compare them to others, although if you are calm and patient they may even swim up to you and sniff your lens.

Penguins all think humans are Leopard Seals! The best way to capture them is to half-submerse yourself in a shallow area and wait – though beware that this can be very cold! With penguins, it is all about patience, as curiosity will eventually get the better of them, and they will swim over to investigate. Gentoos are almost always the most curious, and tend to swim by slowly when you have their attention.

Whales – Humpback or Minke – are generally a difficult mammal to have a good encounter with, as they are big and move quickly. It is really only worth getting in the water with whales when you can stay together as a large group – remember that you cannot encounter a whale, it is the whale that encounters you.

Leopard Seal – the most perfect animal a photographer could wish for – it is a performer and will continue to give a show for hour after hour. As a photographer, you do not need to do anything except for push the shutter release. If you are fortunate enough to have a

Leopard Seal bring you a penguin, stay with it, as the 'Lep' will usually remain only a few meters away, and will come back. However, DO NOT touch the penguin or get too close to the seal. The penguin is its prey and it will feel threatened if it is taken away. Let the seal come to you.

The Underwater World of Antarctica is a place where few in the world will ever personally venture. It has a bountiful benthic and pelagic community, and there are so many opportunities for images while on a dive that it is sometimes difficult to concentrate on only one subject. The key is to keep shooting, and then shoot some more. Whether you are a videographer or photographer, the cost and preparation put into your expedition to Antarctica will all be worthwhile.

Bivalve *Gaimardia trapesina*

Scrumming stars *Decalopoda australis*

Leopard Seal and Gentoo Penguin

Remotely Operated Vehicle (ROV)

In the sub-zero and relatively unexplored bottom of Antarctica waters, ROVs create a scenario whereby a person on the surface, can safely explore at depths of over 100 m. It is often here that unidentified or uncategorized creatures of Antarctica are found.

Remotely Operated Vehicles are just that – there is no operator actually sitting in the vehicle and, instead, a variation of a 'remote control' system is used to drive it. The pilot (they are called this because they 'fly' the ROV) stays dry at the water's surface while the vehicle ventures into the sometimes dangerous underwater environment.

The reason ROVs are typically used in Antarctica is that they enable the human operator to avoid hostile environments in which work needs to be done, or which needs to be explored. Hostile environments come in many forms – low or high temperature, explosive, radioactive, or just plain nasty.

In the beginning, ROVs were used primarily for work deeper than 100 m, but now have also begun to replace divers in shallow water. A few examples are:

- Visual inspection of surface structures such as ships, bridges, and dams.
- Visual inspection of sub-surface structures such as sunken ships or underground water mains.

The bottom-line concerning ROV usage is that divers have physiological limitations that create restrictions as to how long they can stay down, and how deep they can go. Although ROVs do have structural depth limitations, most can stay down for longer and go considerably deeper than even the most advanced divers.

A typical Underwater ROV has at least four major components:

1. The underwater capable vehicle and its components (*e.g.* video camera, sonar, manipulating arm).
2. A handling system that gets the vehicle in and out of the water.
3. The remote control console that remains above the water.
4. A cable and telemetry system linking the vehicle with the control console.

Typically ROVs are used for:

- Searching for and recovery of ship and aircraft wreckage.
- Ocean floor surveys for scientific studies.
- The burial and/or repair of undersea telecommunication cables.
- Support for deep-ocean oil and gas drilling, and production operations.
- Clearance, port and vessel protection, and homeland security.
- Environmental monitoring, scientific exploration, and marine archaeology.

Above: Flying the ROV using the remote control console. Below: Deploying the ROV.

Splash Camera (Splash Cam)

There are times when getting into the water in Antarctica is either not feasible or would be a foolish venture to pursue. Yet, looking out upon the scenario, whether there are Humpback Whales cruising nearby, or a Leopard Seal patroling, it is hard to resist the temptation, even if it is a futile effort to try and keep up with these animals. This is where a Splash Cam comes in handy.

A Splash Cam is a camera inside a protective waterproof housing. This camera is mounted onto a pole, 1–4 m in length, and is lowered into the water to film a particular subject. In most Splash Cam set-ups, the camera that goes in the water is completely separate from the camera that is doing the recording. The hybrid coaxial cable running from the in-water camera comes back onto shore, or into the boat, and is linked to a video camera that records continuously while the camera is submerged. Camera direction is controlled by swiveling the pole in the direction of focus.

The camera can also be dropped into the water without the pole, playing out the coaxial cable until the desired depth is reached. However, keep in mind this will limit the directional control of the camera. Splash Cams usually come with about 50 meters of cable, although cable extensions are available.

Rather than buying the store model, there are ways to make your own Splash Cam. As long as you have an underwater housing for your video or stills camera there is nothing to stop you. Once in the underwater housing, the simplest way of deploying your camera is to place the camera submerged at the water's edge where a flurry of activity is taking place – such as penguins coming and going. For video cameras, the camera can run continuously while gathering images, but for stills cameras, this method will involve manually depressing the shutter or a remote control. Be sure to keep a careful eye on your camera, as it could become dislodged from its resting place, and fall deeper into the sea.

A slightly more complicated method for creating your own Splash Cam is to fashion your own pole, and devise a way of attaching it to your camera housing. Duct Tape is always useful to have available for this purpose.

Dunking

Another way that you can use your own camera as a Splash Cam is to simply dunk it over the side of the Zodiac into the water – in an Underwater Housing of course! This method requires several factors to coincide: good visibility, usually found in the early season; an encounter with an animal that is keen to spend time with you and your Zodiac; the agreement of the expedition naturalists; and adherence to the *Marine Wildlife Watching Guidelines* (see *page 126*). If everything falls into place, then simply submerge your camera within its housing from the most comfortable position you can find (I find that bracing myself against the pontoon offers the greatest stability while still allowing movement). Try different methods of shooting: below the water, half-and-half shots, and shots with flash. All three of these methods can create fantastic and memorable images. However, if you are going to try dunking, I highly recommend waterproof gloves that go to mid-forearm in order to protect your hands from the cold water.

COMMON BENTHIC LIFE OF THE ANTARCTIC PENINSULA AND SOUTH GEORGIA

Edited by Dr. Dennis Cornejo

The benthic life of Antarctica is surprisingly rich. Some of the marine life most likely to be encountered by a recreational diver is shown in this section.

Echinoderms (including sea stars, sea sucumbers, brittle stars and sea urchins)

Sea stars are one of the most common and diverse invertebrates you will notice while diving in Antarctica and South Georgia. They inhabit a wide variety of environments and depths, regulated primarily by what they feed on. Some sea stars are grazers, eating detritus and algae, some utilize larger decaying bodies, and some only feed on sponges or other sea stars. The two most commonly seen species are *Odonaster validus* and *Diplaserias brucei*. *Odonaster validus* is an omnivore that will consume virtually anything it encounters, including detritus, seal feces and even other sea stars. They are often seen in large tightly packed feeding groups or scrums, from which this species gets its colloquial name 'scrumming star'.

Antarctic sea cucumbers are of the 'blooming' type, rather than the type that resemble overgrown slugs. When these 'blooming' cucumbers open up, usually with between 10–30 tentacles surrounding the mouth, they can resemble a flower. The sea cucumbers in the Antarctic region come in a variety of sizes and colors and can be found in a range of habitats. Some may be buried in the substrate, with little more than their mouths and tentacles exposed, while others perch on rocks, sand, shells or algal fronds. Sea cucumbers are filter feeders, catching food that lands on their tentacles. In very slow motion, one tentacle at a time is inserted into the mouth, cleaned of food and then retracted ready to capture more. Sea cucumbers are found generally at depths deeper than 10 m where there are currents, or on walls where detritus falls from above. Sea cucumbers found in South Georgia are smaller than from Antarctica.

Sea star *Odonaster validus*

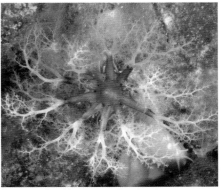

Sea cucumber *Heterocucumis steineni*

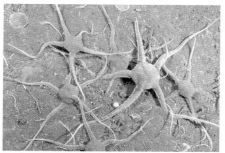
Brittle star *Ophionotus victoriae*

Sea urchin *Sterechinus neumayeri*

Brittle stars in Antarctica inhabit a variety of seabed environments, from rocky pebbles to soft mud, but are only found at certain locations on the peninsula and South Georgia. Where they do occur they can be found at incredibly high densities. Brittle stars are the fastest moving of the echinoderms, using their long arms to propel themselves across the sea floor when startled. Alternatively, they are also able to use these long arms to hold themselves above undesirable substrates and to extricate themselves from heavy falls of marine snow. The two most common species in the peninsula, *Ophiosparte gigas* and *Ophionotus victoriae*, are opportunistic predators and often cannibalistic. A large brittle star can hold down a smaller individual and will clip off all its arms before consuming the central disk!

The most common **sea urchin** in the peninsula is *Sterechinus neumayeri*, which also occurs in South Georgia, but is not as common there. These small urchins are often covered with limpet shells, small stones or toxic red algal fronds, reputedly as protection from predatory sea anemones. When the urchin senses the anemones' tentacles on its 'hat', it will release it hold on the shells, stones or algae and 'dash' to safety. Although primarily herbivorous, this urchin will also graze on any small animal it encounters.

Gastropods (including limpets and nudibranchs)

Limpets are probably the most common benthic invertebrate you will find in the region. Limpets are one of the first creatures to re-inhabit an area after scouring by icebergs, grazing on tiny invertebrates and algae as they travel. The most common species in the region is the Antarctic Limpet *Nacella concinna*. During winter these limpets migrate to deeper water to avoid fast ice. Many individuals' shells are colonized by calcareous red algae that take advantage of this migratory behavior to ensure their own winter survival. Although in peninsula waters they are generally only found in the first 10 m, in South Georgia you will see limpets at all depths in rich benthic environments, especially on kelp. The southern range of the Kelp Gull is most likely defined by the availability of limpets.

Antarctic Limpet *Nacella concinna*

Sea urchin *Sterechinis neumayeri* with 'hats', including Antarctic Limpet *Nacella concinna*.

Nudibranch *Austrodoris kerguelensis*

Nudibranch *Notaeolidia subgigas*

Nudibranchs are shell-less snails, and come in a variety of shapes and forms. Although not always visible, they have rhinophores and gills that protrude from their bodies, making them distinct from other gastropods. However, when frightened they can retract these organs, so approach especially carefully if you would like to take a photograph. Although nudibranchs feed on a variety of organisms, such as sponges and cnidarians, each species is usually adapted to utilize just one or a narrow range of food sources. Sponge-feeding nudibranchs are known to use the sponge's toxic chemicals in their own defense against other predators. Similarly, those that feed on stinging anemones can capture the stinging cells and deploy them as a predator deterrent. Nudibranchs range in size from 10 cm long to no bigger than a fingernail, so they often need careful investigation to locate. It is generally in the most biologically rich dive sites where you will find them.

Ascidians (including tunicates and salps)

There are many types of ascidian in the region's waters. Whilst some are single organisms, others are colonial. They can be either sessile and/or pelagic depending on the species.

Tunicates are by far the most common ascidian, or sea squirt, you will encounter in the region. They are sessile filter feeders, inhabiting areas with currents or an ample supply of detritus. Although tunicates have been recorded in water up to 150 m deep, they need a rich environment in which to feed, and so they are generally only found in areas where ice does not consistently hinder their development, *i.e.* vertical walls, and protected overhangs.

Tunicate *Cnemidocarpa verrucosa*

Worms

Almost all environments and depths in Antarctica and South Georgia are inhabited by worms. They come in a variety of sizes and shapes, resembling anything from fine embroidery thread to thick heaving line. Many are filter feeders living in rich areas undisturbed by ice, while others feed on detritus and decaying material, living under rocks to gain protection from the large icebergs that scour the sea floor. Photographers need to approach slowly, as some of the worms can spook very easily, pulling back into their protective holes or tubes.

Fish (including Notothenids)

Unlike in tropical regions where one cannot help but be inundated by fish, in Antarctica fish are few and far between. One reason for their elusiveness is that Antarctic species generally do not possess a swim bladder and are therefore rarely seen swimming. They are usually found lying motionless on the seabed, quite often remaining so until a diver is nearly on top of them. For this reason, if you approach slowly and keep a safe distance they are quite easy to photograph. Fish in the region can be found at any dive site – if you look closely enough.

Worm *Flabelligera mundata*

Nemertean worm *Parbolasis corrugata*

Nothothenid fish *Notothenia rossii*

Young notothenid fish

Cnidarians (including anemones, hydroids, jellyfish, and soft corals)

Although there are many 'stinging animals' in Antarctica, even if you came in very close contact, it is doubtful you would be stung as diving apparel and equipment afford good protection.

Anemones are the most common cnidarian you will encounter. Anemones in Antarctica exhibit a broad variety of sizes, shapes, and color. As most are filter feeders they do not re-colonize scour zones quickly, and you will mostly find them in areas with currents that also offer protection from major changes to their environment. They can be found on rocky or soft substrate, and some even burrow, although these species are usually found well below diving depths. In South Georgia, most of the anemones are smaller and more delicate, looking like tiny flowers lining the holdfasts of the kelp.

Sea anemone *Isotella antarctica*

Soft corals are some of the most beautiful and dainty animals in Antarctica and South Georgia. The same species are found in both regions, generally under ledges and in other areas where the animals can remain undisturbed, but with enough water flow to allow filter feeding.

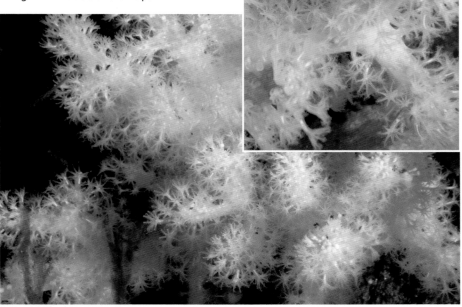

Soft coral *Alcyonium antarcticum*

Sponges

Sponges are usually found on walls or overhangs that are protected from ice scouring and strong light, but are also well served with nutrient rich currents. Because of these requirements, the 'sponge zone' is usually found below 10 m. However, in areas like the east side of the Antarctic Peninsula, which encounters massive ice disruption at depths as great as 100 m, sponge colonies are usually sparse and found at extreme depths. Sponges in Antarctica and South Georgia come in a variety of shapes, sizes, and colors. Food for many species of invertebrate, they also have commensalistic relationships with other species, such as worms that often make homes in their oscula (large openings).

Algae

Although you can find red and green algae in the region, most of what you will see are brown algae. These mainly marine species come in a variety of sizes and shapes, and include the largest algae in the region. Small clusters of algae are generally found as early colonizers of areas recently scoured by ice. While diving on walls, or areas otherwise protected from ice, you will notice that the algae are more plentiful and larger in size. The largest alga in Antarctica is the Large-frond Tang *Himantothallus grandifolius* with a blade 8 m long and a meter wide, which can literally carpet a site. In South Georgia you will encounter the Giant Kelp *Macrocystis pyrifera*, the same species that forms the famous kelp forests of California, which

Sponge growth with several species of sponge

can grow as tall as 30 m. Within and underneath larger algae are quite often good places to look for delicate organisms that are gaining protection and reaching zones of higher elevation within the water column.

Sea spiders

Although they resemble terrestrial spiders, sea spiders are actually closely related to horseshoe crabs. The largest of the sea spiders has been recorded in Antarctica, where some grow to over 40 cm, although the vast majority are smaller, 10–20 cm, and sometimes difficult to spot. Sea spiders are slow movers, and as such they remain close to their source of food, which includes sponges, hydroids, and bryozoans. As pictured below, a male sea spider carries its eggs using an additional pair of legs (ovigers).

Kelp

Sea spider *Ammothea carolinensis* – male carrying eggs

NATURAL PRODUCT CHEMISTRY FROM ANTARCTIC MARINE ORGANISMS

Bill J. Baker – Center for Drug Discovery and Innovation

The stark white landscape of terrestrial Antarctica and gentle blue-green hues of glacial ice contrasts sharply with the marine environment. Underwater, forests of red, green and brown seaweeds rival the kelp forests of the Pacific, colorful invertebrates carpet rocky substrates in a tapestry of delightful complexity, and the activity of fishes, seals and penguins belies the notion of Antarctica as a serene environment. Indeed, Antarctica has been encircled by the circumpolar current for millennia, establishing an endemic marine flora and fauna protected from encroachment by organisms from other continents by extreme cold and unusual patterns of day and night. These endemic seaweeds and animals have used those millennia to develop relationships among themselves: some as predators, some as prey, some as fast-growing 'weedy' competitors for space, and some as purveyors of noxious or toxic defensive chemicals. Such interactions underlie Antarctic chemical ecology, a field of science that seeks to understand how the benthic community structure is influenced by these chemical products of nature, so-called natural products.

The contrast between life above and below the high tide line is striking.
ABOVE: The view from the surface of the ocean looking toward Eichorst Island near Palmer Station, Antarctica, and its bleak, uninhabited landscape. BELOW: Reds, yellows and blues color sea life a mere three meters below that same surface.

Antarctic chemical ecology is dominated by the predominant organisms, the large brown algae, known commonly as seaweeds. These algae produce natural product chemicals that are distasteful to local fishes and so manage to escape predation. In many parts of the world, fish predation is a major factor that limits algal growth. In an interesting twist of fate, in Antarctica it is the smallest predator that inflicts the most damage to these algae: tiny shrimp-like creatures known as amphipods. Amphipods are not much larger than a flea, but are found in enormous numbers – as many as 300,000 per square meter of seafloor – bringing to mind the ancient Chinese torture, 'death by 1,000 cuts'. But in reality, the amphipods and algae live in a dynamic relationship where the amphipods primarily feed on small fungal or microalgal colonies on the surface of the seaweeds, and the algae actually provide a haven for the amphipods from the fish that predate them.

Benthic marine invertebrates of Antarctica similarly benefit from fishes who prefer amphipods and other crustaceans. This is one aspect of Antarctic ecology that differs

Even though the keystone predators in some parts of Antarctica are tiny, their large numbers demand a strategy from potential prey. LEFT: A large gathering of amphipods grazing on diatoms growing on the surface of seaweed. RIGHT: A lone amphipod near the back of a mollusk, among seaweed *Himanthothallus*.

considerably from temperate and tropical marine ecology, where fish are the dominant predators. Instead, on the Antarctic seafloor, sponges and tunicates and other benthic invertebrates must protect themselves from sea star predators. Sea stars may be slow, but the invertebrates they eat, like terrestrial plants, are attached to the ground and so they cannot flee the menacing sea stars. One sponge, known commonly as the Green Sponge, was found to concentrate toxic natural product chemicals in its surface tissue. This is effective against the sea stars because they feed by pushing their stomach out of their body cavity and onto their prey, digesting it rather than biting it. The chemicals concentrated on the surface of the Green Sponge therefore protect it from sea star predation.

Tunicates can take on the appearance of a sponge, although they are about as related to sponges as are humans. But like sponges, tunicates need a defensive strategy against sea star predation. One of the most common tunicates produces a suite of defensive natural product toxins, perhaps optimizing each one against a different predator. These toxins are known as the palmerolides, the name being derived from the scientific research station where they were discovered, Palmer Station, appended to a suffix that describes the chemical class known as macrolides to which the toxins belong,

Perhaps it is not surprising that many natural products have properties as human drugs. In fact, most pharmaceutical drugs on the market are either natural products or are derived

Antarctic marine organisms use a variety of chemical strategies for survival.
LEFT: The Green Sponge *Latrunculia apicalis* concentrates toxins near its surface to deter predation by sea stars. RIGHT: A sea star *Odontaster* sp. feeding on seaweed (note the stomach protruding from the sea star's body cavity as its feeding mechanism).

Palmerolide A displays potent and selective activity against melanoma (shown here with the tunicate *Synoicum adareanum* from which it was discovered).

from natural products. One of the palmerolide natural products is being studied as an anticancer drug. That the palmerolides are toxins may imply that they should be excluded from consideration for use as human drugs. However, many drugs are toxins and are selected based on their ability to kill cells, such as cancer cells or the cells of an infectious agent, such as a bacterium or fungus. The special feature of a toxin that makes it a likely drug is that it is more toxic to the disease-causing cell than it is to healthy human cells. Natural products are excellent drug candidates precisely because they have evolved in living organisms for the express purpose of targeting a specific cell or part of a cell, and that selectivity can often be exploited for human benefit.

Nudibranchs are mollusks not unlike the common slugs found in gardens. These sea slugs lack a protective shell, are ponderously slow, and specialize their diet on particular food items, such as sponges or seaweeds, much as a garden slug might prefer tomatoes over cabbages. Nudibranchs differ from garden slugs in sporting a large gill on their back for extracting oxygen from the water. Often brightly colored, and with an intricately complex gill on one end and antennae-like appendage at the other, nudibranchs are stunningly beautiful animals. *Austrodoris*, a white-to-orange nudibranch common in Antarctica, has used natural products in a manner that facilitated the evolution of new types of nudibranchs. It is believed that during geologic periods when glaciers extended into the sea around continental Antarctica, the nudibranchs were separated into pockets, bound on each side by ice. The nudibranchs in each pocket faced different groups of predators and as a consequence developed slightly different natural product chemicals for defence. When the glaciers retreated, such as during the current geologic period, the various groups of nudibranch were free to move. Although the result was mixed assemblages, each group retained its own arsenal of defensive chemicals. The variety of chemical signals that can be detected today are therefore a relic of previous glacial periods.

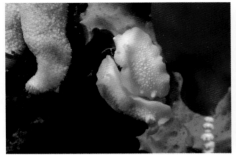

Antarctic sea slugs. LEFT: Two *Austrodoris* nudibranchs frolic on their favorite sponge, *Dendrilla*. RIGHT: The Frilly Nudibranch on its favorite meal, a calcareous bryozoan.

Among the more unusual mollusks in Antarctica are the swimming slugs, commonly referred to as sea butterflies due to the similarity of their 'flight' behaviour. Sea butterflies, scientifically called pteropods, have evolved wing-like appendages (thus *ptero*, from the ancient Greek for wing) from the part of the mollusk normally used for locomotion, referred to as the mollusk's foot (thus *pod*, again from the Greek). So these 'winged foot' mollusks seemingly fly through the water column, and a diver finding themself in the midst of a swarm of sea butterflies could easily forget they are underwater, appearing instead to be in a field on a summer afternoon surrounded by butterflies. The Antarctic pteropod known as *Clione antarctica* has developed a natural product defence since, like the seafloor-living shell-less mollusks, they need protection from fish predation. In an unprecedented state of affairs, *Clione* sea butterflies can be abducted by amphipods. *Clione* is held in place on the amphipod's back so the amphipod can itself be protected from fish predation due to the chemical cargo it is carrying. Other pteropods, such as *Limicina*, have shells, like garden snails, and therefore are less dependent upon chemical defences.

The Antarctic marine environment is indeed a rich and varied source of biodiversity, much of which uses natural products chemistry in one form or another for interactions among community members. Because of the unique geology, including regular periods of glaciers extending into the sea, the harsh physical environment where liquid water cannot get any colder lest it solidifies, and the extended remoteness, separated as it has been for tens of millions of years from the rest of the globe by the circumpolar current, Antarctic marine invertebrates and seaweeds have evolved ecological interrelationships unlike those found elsewhere. From icefish living without red-pigmented haemoglobin in their blood and awesome coral-like animals that look like no animal you have ever seen, to slugs that swim with the fish, life at the end of the world sometimes seems otherworldly. Perhaps these otherworldly natural products will one day impact the distinctly worldly cause in the service of human health.

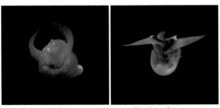

The swimming mollusks of Antarctica. LEFT: The pteropod *Clione antarctica* madly flapping its 'wings' to propel itself through the water column. RIGHT: The pteropod *Limicina limicina* swimming gracefully.

Weird and wonderful creatures of Antarctica. TOP: The Blackfin Icefish *Chaenocephalus aceratus* is nearly transparent due to blood that lacks haemoglobin pigmentation. BOTTOM: Despite its appearance, *Candelabrum penola*, pictured here, is most closely related to corals.

How to use this guide

The bulk of this book is devoted to providing information, descriptions, and guidance on the diving conditions at 24 dive sites on the Antarctic Peninsula and seven on South Georgia. The map opposite indicates the location of each of the Peninsula dive sites, numbered broadly from north to south, and the map on *page 109.* shows the dive sites on South Georgia, numbered from east to west.

Each dive site account is structured in a similar way and includes its coordinates and a map showing the approximate position of each dive location (indicated with a flag ◄).

Towards the top of the account is a series of icons that provide a quick summary of the key features of the site, including its nature, the likelihood of currents and surges, and the presence of Leopard Seals or penguins. A key to the icons used is given below.

The maximum depth of the dive site and information on likely issues with ice are given in a shaded blue box, together with an indication of the wildlife that may be encountered at different depths.

The main text contains a section on 'conditions', which provides more detail on the site, where to go and what to look for, and, importantly, the potential hazards. Where appropriate, special notes are included in shaded red boxes to highlight particular aspects of the site.

Each dive site account is illustrated with a series of photographs of some of the species or features that are likely to be seen. The section on the *Common benthic life of the Antarctic Peninsula and South Georgia* on *pages 44–52* provides more detailed information on the types of animals that occur in these waters.

Key to icons used in the guide

The following icons provide a quick summary of the features of a dive site.

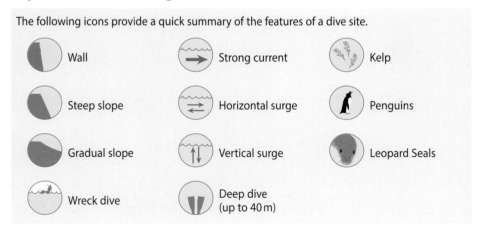

Wall

Steep slope

Gradual slope

Wreck dive

Strong current

Horizontal surge

Vertical surge

Deep dive
(up to 40 m)

Kelp

Penguins

Leopard Seals

DIVE SITES OF THE ANTARCTIC PENINSULA

Palmer Station, USA

Jubany, Argentina, Germany
King Sejong, Korea

Yelcho Station, Chile

Rothera Station, UK

ANTARCTIC PENINSULA

Scott Base, New Zealand

McMurdo Station, USA/Canada

Terra Nova Mario Zucchelli Station, Italy

Dumont d'Urville, France

Casey, Australia

ANTARCTICA

60°S

Elephant Island **1**

62°S

Aitcho Islands **6**

SOUTH SHETLAND ISLANDS

2 Tay Head

7
8 **9** Deception Island

3 Paulet Island

65°W

Mikkelsen Harbor **10**

Hydruga Rocks **11**

55°W

60°W

64°S **4** Bald Head

5 Cape Well-met

Janus Island Arthur Harbor **18**

Booth Island **19**

Plenéau Island **20**

Petermann Island **21**

12 Enterprise Islands

13 Orne Harbor

14 Cuverville Island

15 Neko Harbor

16 Paradise Harbor

17 Port Lockroy

Prospect Point **22**

ANTARCTIC PENINSULA

Detaille Island **23**

WEDDELL SEA

Larsen Ice Shelf

Kilometers

0   50   100   150   200

Stonington Island **24**

Depth:
Up to 18 m

Ice:
Brash Ice can be a factor to be contended with, as the nearby glacier is very active. There also may be bergy bits grounded or floating about Point Wild, preventing or making access to the dive site difficult.

What you might see:
TOP **7** M:
Sea stars
Limpets
Algae

BELOW **7** M:
Sea stars
Tunicates
Anemones
Algae
Sea spiders
Notothenids

Elephant Island is the easternmost outlier of the South Shetland Islands. It was discovered and chartered by Edward Bransfield, RN in 1820, and was named for the many Southern Elephant Seals found there. Most notably this is the first *terra firma* Shackleton and the men of his *Endurance* expedition landed upon after escaping the ice. Point Wild was named for Frank Wild, the leader of the 22 men who were stranded here for 135 days while Shackleton made a desperate attempt to find help. Thankfully, on 30 August 1916 the men on Elephant Island were rescued after a two-year battle of survival against the Southern Ocean.

CONDITIONS
Elephant Island is fully exposed to the Southern ocean and all its forces, and Point Wild offers little reprieve from a constant battering of surge from the North. This surge can make diving difficult and very dangerous.

It is not uncommon for divers at this site to lose spatial bearings, reach an undesired depth, or abort the dive because of a combination of adverse conditions. The dive should only be attempted in relatively calm conditions, which unfortunately are rare around the island.

Due to surge, it is necessary to hug the wall upon descent and ascent. The upper 3 m of the wall are often scoured by brash ice and bergy bits which have broken off of the nearby glacier, or grounded icebergs trapped around the island. However, below 7 m a good variety of life is present.

Point Wild, Elephant Island

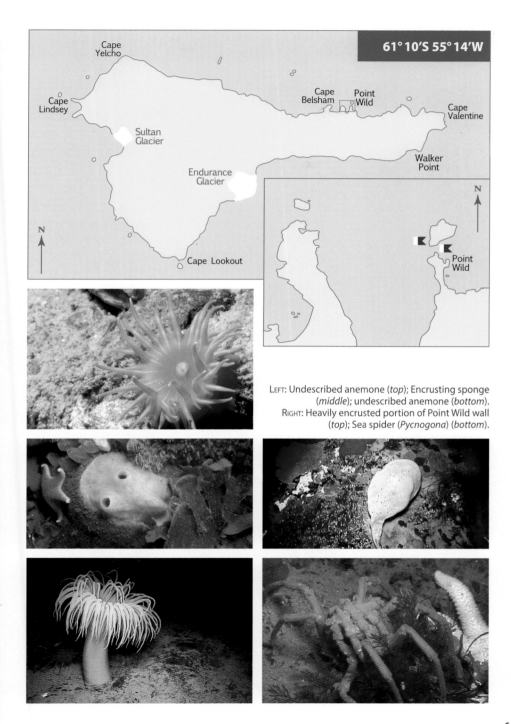

Cape Yelcho

Cape Lindsey

Cape Belsham

Point Wild

Cape Valentine

Sultan Glacier

Endurance Glacier

Walker Point

N

Cape Lookout

N

Point Wild

LEFT: Undescribed anemone (*top*); Encrusting sponge (*middle*); undescribed anemone (*bottom*).
RIGHT: Heavily encrusted portion of Point Wild wall (*top*); Sea spider (*Pycnogona*) (*bottom*).

Tay Head is a rocky headland 10 km east of Mount Alexander, extending into the Firth of Tay on the south coast of Joinville Island. The name was given by a UK Antarctic exploration expedition (1963), derived from the Firth of Tay, which is a 20 km sound between Dundee Island and Joinville Island, named for the Firth of Tay of Scotland.

CONDITIONS

The dive site lies off the eastern side of Tay Head, and is marked by the rocky stacks which protrude from the water there. It is good to be aware that there can be a current here, so take the time to observe any obvious signs while still on the surface. Even though this is an easy sloping bottom, it is suggested that divers enter the water where the bottom can be seen. Upon entry it is a gradual slope which becomes steeper the further you descend, continuing past diving depth. This slope really demonstrates the different levels and resilience of the benthic life of Antarctica. The first 8 m are scoured quite heavily by ice, so only limpets and urchins are visible. Then, as you descend deeper past the 10 m mark, life becomes more abundant, with sponges to be found in the cracks, and single brightly colored anemones in the middle of a barren white rock. The water column may also have some interesting pelagic life, such as jellyfish and ctenophores.

Depth:
Up to 40 m

Ice:
There is almost always ice in this area from the Weddell Sea, and the active glaciers near by.

What you might see:
TOP **8 M:**
Algae
Small notothenids
Urchins
Sea stars
Limpets

BELOW **8 M:**
Tunicates
Anemones
Notothenids
Sponges

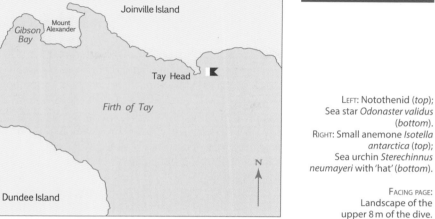

LEFT: Notothenid (*top*); Sea star *Odonaster validus* (*bottom*).
RIGHT: Small anemone *Isotella antarctica* (*top*); Sea urchin *Sterechinnus neumayeri* with 'hat' (*bottom*).

FACING PAGE: Landscape of the upper 8 m of the dive.

Paulet Island lies south of Dundee Island at the southern tip of the Trinity Peninsula. It was discovered by Captain J.C. Ross in 1842, and named for a fellow naval captain, The Right Honourable Lord George Paulet, RN. On shore there is a large Adelie Penguin colony, and the remains of the stone hut in which Captain C.A. Larsen and the crew of *Antarctic* over-wintered in 1903. Today a commemorative plaque is in place, and an accessible metal fence surrounds the hut to prevent penguins from nesting on the ruins.

CONDITIONS

During the 2003–04 season, Paulet was not reached by ship until mid-January due to extreme ice conditions in the Weddell Sea. Although each year the ice is variable, it is a good idea to keep up-to-date with the current ice conditions when planning for your dive expeditions.

Due to currents bringing ice from further south in the Weddell Sea, Paulet's entire shore can be encased in ice, making diving impossible. Even when diving is possible, there can be a strong tidal current that moves the ice into the dive site during the dive, disrupting entry and exit. The further away from shore a diver ventures, the stronger this current becomes.

The shallow, rocky, and relatively organism free bottom closer to shore is known as the scour zone. This area changes from week to week as ice moves in and out from shore. The ice scrapes the bottom free from any colonizing benthos. For this reason, in the first 9 m of water, you find very little life. What you do find are the faster-moving, hearty, and resilient animals such as limpets, urchins, and amphipods.

Depth:
6–24 m

Ice:
There are often grounded icebergs close to shore, shedding large bergy bits and brash ice, which can completely block the shore.

What you might see:
Algae
Limpets
Sea stars
Sea urchins
Amphipods
Brittle stars
Small notothenids
Worms
Possibility of Adelie
  Penguins swimming
  through the water
Possibility of Weddell
  Seals

Special Note: During the fledging period for Adelie Penguin chicks in late January and early February, there can be many Leopard Seals patrolling the shoreline. The newly fledged chicks still have some down, which makes it difficult for them to submerge themselves, creating an easy target for the Leopard Seal. The Leopard Seals on this side of the peninsula seem to be less habituated to Zodiacs and divers, and usually keep their distance. However, they are inherently curious and there is always an exception to the rule, so be cautious.

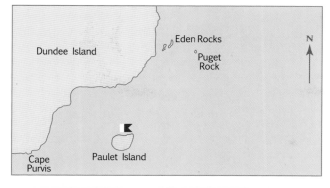

Left: Weddell Seal
Leptonychotes weddelli (*above*);
Icebergs scraping on the
seabed create the scour zone at
Paulet Island (*below*);
Right: The remains of the stone
hut in which Captain Larsen
and the crew of the *Antarctic*
over-wintered (*top*);
scour zone (*bottom*).

65

To 12 m

ROV site

Bald Head is a point of land located on the south side of the Trinity peninsula, and was first seen in 1902–03 by J. Gunnar Andersson's party under Nordenskjöld's Expedition.

CONDITIONS

There are two dive sites here: a shallow site reaching a maximum depth of 12 m, and a deep site where the outer limits (40 m) of recreational diving can be reached.

The shallow site is regularly scoured by icebergs, leaving the gradually sloping bottom of small and medium sized rocks relatively bare. There are often small icebergs grounded close to shore and, during times of good visibility, it is easy to observe how they are positioned, as well as to take clear photos without getting too close. Do take care not to approach the icebergs closer than the recommended 'twice the height above the water', as all icebergs can split or turn unexpectedly.

Although I have never dived deeper than 12 m here, through ROV exploration and colleagues' accounts, the deeper waters are within the outer limits of recreational diving, and contrast sharply with the shallower areas of the site. The bottom slopes away drastically to reach depths greater than 40 m; the landscape becoming full of large boulders, revealing a spectacular bottom, full of life.

Depth:
Up to 40 m

Ice:
Early in the season, there are often large ice floes in the area, and almost always grounded icebergs near the dive site.

What you might see:
Algae
Limpets
Sea stars
Sea urchins

ROV DIVE TO **40 M:**
Anemones
Tunicates
Crinoids
Sea spiders
Sponges
Hydroids

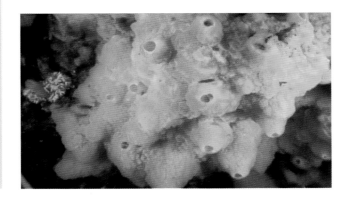

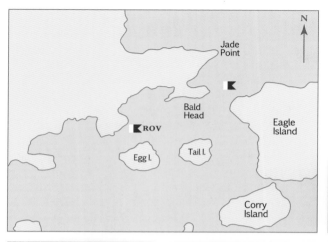

Top: Amphipod *Antarcturus mawsoni*; Middle: Antarctic Limpet *Nacella concinna* (*left*); Comb jelly *Beroe cucumis* (*center*); Sea urchin *Sterurchinus neumayeri* with crinoid *Promachocrinus kerguelensis* as a 'hat' (*right*) Bottom: Crinoid *Promachocrinus kerguelensis*.

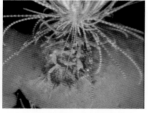

67

Cape Well-met is a dark conspicuous headland on the north side of Vega Island. Discovered and named by the Swedish Antarctic Expedition, 1901–04, it was at this spot where the relief party under Dr. J. Gunnar Andersson, and the winter party under Dr. Otto Nordenskjöld, finally rendezvoused after 20 months of forced separation.

CONDITIONS

This wall can be tricky to find, as there is a shelf that extends 100 m out from the Cape face, at only 3–7 m of depth. It can make for an unusually long swim if you misjudge the entrance point. In order to make the most efficient and safe drop for the site, it is suggested that you enter the water due east of the Cape tip, then swim north until you meet the wall. However it is important that divers drop where they can still see the bottom, as especially in times of poor visibility, if you do not follow the flat shelf, you may miss the wall completely. Keep in mind that this shelf, although tedious to swim over in the beginning, is a perfect spot for the safety stop.

Upon reaching the wall, it is a spectacular drop into the sheer blue. The wall is undisturbed by ice, and is completely covered in life. Be sure to look not only at the immediate creatures in view, such as anemones, but also what may be on top of them, such as sea spiders and nudibranchs.

Depth:
Up to 40 m

Ice:
In the early season this area can still have fast ice attached to the surrounding islands, and there are almost always bergy bits and brash ice whatever the time of year.

What you might see:
TOP **5 M:**
Sea stars
Limpets
Algae

BELOW **10 M:**
Sea stars
Tunicates
Anemones
Sea spiders
Sponged
Notothenids
Nudibranchs

Special Note: This is one of the most spectacular wall dives around the Antarctic Peninsula. I have explored this area by ROV and know that this wall drops to over 100 m almost straight down, so it can be a bit daunting (and exciting) for individuals. Complete control of buoyancy is an absolute must on this dive.

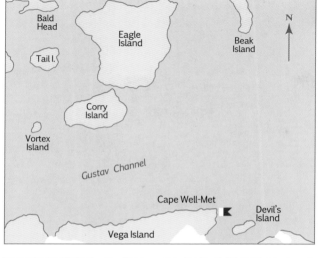

Bald Head

Eagle Island

Beak Island

Tail I.

N

Corry Island

Vortex Island

Gustav Channel

Cape Well-Met

Devil's Island

Vega Island

LEFT: Notothenid *Notothenia rossii* (*top*); Soft coral *Alcyonium antarcticum* (*bottom*). RIGHT: Entaculate ctenophore (*top*); Looking down the wall at Cape Well-met (*bottom*).

FACING PAGE: Tunicate *Molgula pendunculata*.

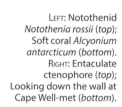

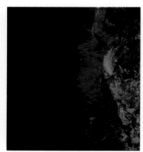

This small group of islands lies within the English Strait, the body of water separating Robert and Greenwich Islands, in the South Shetland Islands. They are so named from the initials of the British Hydrographic Office (HO). Covered extensively with moss, they are also home to Gentoo and Chinstrap Penguins.

Cecilia and Barrientos Islands are the southernmost of the Aitcho Islands.

CONDITIONS

All the dive sites have a very strong tidal current, which can sweep you out from land, away from your boat, and towards the center of English Strait by as much as 1 km. It is suggested that divers use the walls and slopes as reference points during ascent and descent. On most occasions there is also surge at the dive sites, especially on the northern coasts of the islands, which are exposed to the swells of the Drake Passage. This can disrupt safety stops and cause divers to become disorientated. However, this surge usually dies down after 5 m, allowing a smooth dive to depth.

Depth:
Up to 40 m

Ice:
Ice is usually not a factor, but there may be a few bergy bits floating close to shore.

What you might see:
TOP **7** M:
Limpets
Sea stars
Kelp
Algae
Small snails
Can be scoured in places due to the icebergs that move in and out of the English Straight

BELOW **7** M:
Small notothenids
Sea cucumbers
Hydroids
Sun stars
Feather coral
Basketball sponges
Anemones
Nudibranchs
Sea spiders

IN THE WATER COLUMN:
Colonial salps
Pteropods

Special Note: There are frequently Leopard Seals in these areas, especially around Barrientos Island. Habituated to Zodiacs, these animals are often very curious of boats and divers, encircling or even nudging to investigate their underwater visitors.

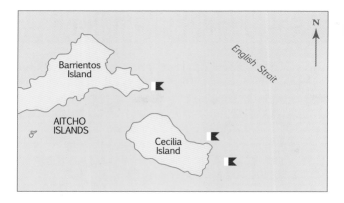

LEFT: Sea cucumber *Cucumaria* sp.;
RIGHT: Entaculate ctenophore (*top*);
Polychete worm *Flabelligera mundata*. (*middle*);
Pteropod *Clione* (*bottom*).

FACING PAGE: Colonial salp.

The shallow, rocky, and relatively organism-free bottom closer to shore is known as the scour zone. This area changes from week to week as ice moves in and out from shore. The ice scrapes the bottom free from any colonizing benthos. For this reason, in the first 9 m of water, you find very little life. What you do find are the faster-moving, hearty, and resilient animals such as limpets, urchins, and amphipods. At greater depths (15–30 m) larger and unique invertebrates such as nudibranchs, anemones and hydroids can be found.

Deception Island is an active volcano in the South Shetland Islands, which last erupted in 1970, and has a large flooded crater. The caldera is open to the sea through Neptune's Bellows, a narrow passage on the southeast side. This allows ships to enter into the sheltered natural harbor of Port Foster.

There are many historical sites on the island including an old whaling and sealing station, and an abandoned British Research Base. Currently, long-term studies are being done by various countries, which include biological re-colonization and seismic studies. Deception Island is visited by almost every scientific and passenger expedition to the Antarctic Peninsula, often for the sole purpose of allowing the passengers to 'wallow' in the thermally heated water found on the shoreline inside the crater.

There are three dive sites: Sewing Machine Needles, Neptune's Bellows and Whaler's Bay, each of which is described here.

TOP: Brittle star *Ophionotus victoriae* (*left*); Sea star on encrusted wall of 'Sewing Machine Needles'(*right*); BOTTOM: Sea urchins by the thousand line the bottom of Port Foster.

FACING PAGE: Notothenid.

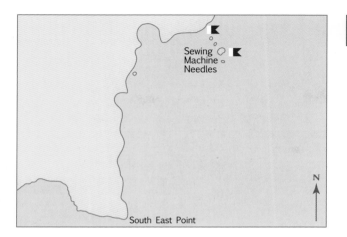

7 SEWING MACHINE NEEDLES

These are three rocky stacks located on the outside of the island, between Neptune's Bellows and Bailey Head. Called 'Sewing Machine Rock' by whalers, for what was originally a natural arch, needles is now considered the better description, as the arch collapsed during an earthquake in 1924.

CONDITIONS

This site is exposed and often rough, especially with a large swell from the southeast.

Dives normally start from the largest and outermost stack, below which there is a stepped wall with shelves at 12 m and 17 m, after which it becomes a steeply sloping wall. The stack meets the seabed at 25 m, and the bottom below this is volcanic rock.

Depth:
11–27 m

Ice:
Rare

What you might see:
FIRST 7 M:
Algae
Limpets
Sea stars

BELOW 7 M:
Sea spiders
Sea stars
Hydroids
Nudibranchs
Moon snails
Notothenids

IN THE WATER COLUMN:
Pteropods
Ctenophores
Chinstraps

73

8 NEPTUNE'S BELLOWS

This 500 m break in the crater wall is the only entrance into the flooded caldera of Deception Island. Invisible from a distance, the entrance appears quite wide as you approach, but due to a large submerged rock sitting only 2 m from the surface in the middle, only half of the opening is navigable. The dive site is found below the steep cliffs on the northeastern side of the narrowest part of the channel.

CONDITIONS

A strong tidal current of 2–3 knots flows through Neptune's Bellows, so it is best to wait until slack tide. Additionally swells from the east may cause significant surge.

The dive starts down a thickly covered algae slope, which becomes a boulder-strewn bottom at 10 m. A coarse gravel slope further descends to the center of the channel. Moving across the slope below 12 m, the pebbles are interspersed by vertical cliffs and rock outcroppings 2–3 m tall. These rocky features and small cracks within them create a protected habitat for some interesting marine creatures.

There is a steep wall, lined with sponges, anemones and tunicates, below the cliffs just before entering Port Foster, but easy to miss when entering the water. I suggest descending more towards the middle of the Bellows to 10 m and following the slope east (keeping the slope on your right) until the wall is met.

Depth:
7–25 m

Ice:
Not a factor.

What you might see:
TOP **6 M:**
Algae
Limpets (on rocks)
Brittle stars

BELOW **6 M:**
Sea urchins
Brittle stars (by the
   thousands)
Anemones
Notothenids
Soft coral
Nudibranchs
Soft-shelled clams
Sponges
Tunicates
Sea spiders

Special Note: It is important to not only check the incoming and outgoing tides, but also the shipping schedules as Deception Island is one of the most frequented spots in Antarctica, and there is daily traffic in and out of Neptune's Bellows. Radio Officers, the AIS (Automatic Identification System), and the IAATO ship schedule are all good sources of information. It would be a disaster to be stuck in the narrow passage while a ship was entering or departing, and has no room to maneuver.

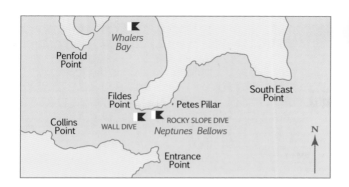

9 WHALER'S BAY

Whaler's Bay is the first bay inside and to the north of Neptune's Bellows, named by French explorer Jean-Baptiste Charcot for the whalers that used the area as an anchorage and shore station. Ashore, there are several derelict buildings, which are remains of the whaling station and a British base. These are protected as historic sites. There is also an Antarctic Specially Protected Area (ASPA) for long-term scientific study around Kroner Lake – the 'green lake' which lies to the south of the buildings. **Do not enter the ASPA** as access is restricted.

CONDITIONS

The water conditions in Whaler's Bay are almost always calm below the surface with no surge. You can do a shore dive, but be aware that the gravely bottom drops off very quickly – 9 m from shore you find yourself in 12 m of water. The sloping bottom makes an easy reference to follow throughout the dive.

Special Note: For most, this dive will most likely occur during a passenger landing at the historical whaling station. Be aware of Zodiac traffic, as the visibility is not sufficient near the surface for boat drivers to see divers, or divers to see them.

Unlike most spots in the Antarctic, here a deeper dive does not reveal more diversity. ROV exploration has shown similar species distributed from 10–70 m.

Depth:
Up to 40 m

Ice:
Not a factor.

Water Temperature:
CLOSE TO SHORE: 5–18°C
This temperature is only found in a small area near the surface and close to shore, due to the mixing of the geothermally warmed water, rising up to mix with the cold water flowing in from the sea.
AT DEPTH: −2 – −1°C

What you might see:
IN UNBELIEVABLE NUMBERS:
Brittle stars
Sea stars
Sea urchins
Worms

OCCASIONALLY:
Anemone
Tunicates
Notothenids

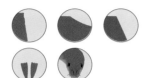

Mikkelsen Harbor is a small bay indenting the south side of Trinity Island that was discovered by the Swedish Antarctic Expedition 1901–04. The origin of the name has not been documented, but was in common usage when the Scottish geologist David Ferguson sailed on the whale-catcher *Hanka* in 1913.

CONDITIONS
The wall portion of this dive site can be difficult to find, so it is important to use landmarks. While looking at the island where the hut lies from the east, position the entry point for the dive between the hut and the shallow reef that sits just off the island. Entering the water, there is a slope down to 10 m, and suddenly the slope gives way to a wall extending down to 24 m, before becoming a gradual slope.

A good draping of algae, both filamentous and fronds, covers the wall. Filter-feeding animals can be found under the algae, and the more mobile invertebrates on the outside of the algae. If the diver should miss the wall, it is paralleled on either side by steep slopes which also have a wide variety of life.

Depth:
24–30 m

Ice:
Aside from a few pieces here and there, ice is generally not a factor.

What you might see:
TOP **10 M:**
Sea stars
Limpets
Algae
Amphipods

BELOW **15 M:**
Sun stars
Nudibranchs
Sponges
Tunicates
Worms
Sea stars
Notothenids

Special Note: A depth finder is a useful piece of equipment for this dive. It will assist in finding where the wall begins, and also ensure the diver does not drop into extremely deep water missing the wall completely.
Leopard Seals are often seen here patrolling the shores for penguins entering and exiting the water.

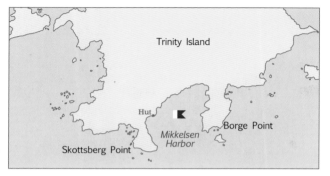

Left: Notothenid *Notothenia rossii* (*top*); A fully extended polychete worm *Potamilla antarctica* (*bottom*).
Right: Sea stars feeding on a Giant Isopod (*top*); Open siphon of a tunicate (*middle*); Closed siphon of a tunicate (*bottom*).

Facing page: A sea cucumber feeds from the water column.

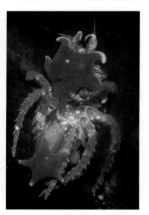

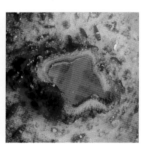

This site consists of a group of rocks lying east of Two Hummock Island, in the Palmer Archipelago. These rocks are named after the scientific name of the Leopard Seal *Hydrurga leptonyx*, although this species of seal is seldom seen in the area.

CONDITIONS

Close to the rocky passenger landing site there is a small pinnacle which rises to just under 3 m below the surface. Easily identified on marine charts, it slopes downward to a sandy bottom at just under 27 m. This pinnacle creates a natural reference for the dive.

The pinnacle slopes steeply to a sandy plateau that is covered in areas by small groups of algae. Sharply contrasting with the normally rocky dive sites of the Antarctic Peninsula, the sandy bottom offers a sparsely populated, but resilient benthic community.

The water column surrounding this rock can hold some of the smallest, but nonetheless, interesting creatures such as small pteropods and ctenophores, so make sure to look around during ascent and descent.

Depth:
27 m

Ice:
Aside from a few small pieces floating on the surface, ice has not been a factor.

What you might see:
IN THE WATER COLUMN:
Ctenopohores
Salps
Pteropods
Jellyfish

ON THE SEABED:
Amphipods
Worms
Notothenids
Sea stars
Anemones

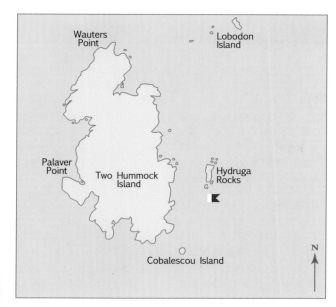

LEFT: Cnidarian
Diplumaris antarctica
RIGHT: Colonial salp (*top*);
Anemone *Isotella antarctica*
(*bottom*).

FACING PAGE: Nemertean worms
Parbolasia corrugata.

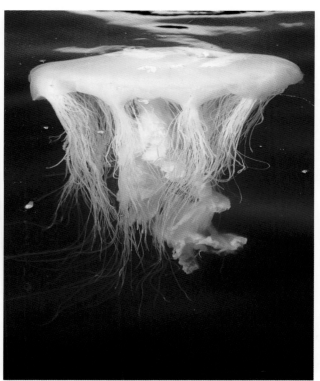

ENTERPRISE ISLANDS, *GOVERNØREN* WRECK

The Enterprise Islands lay in Wilhelmina Bay, which is located at the northeastern end of Nansen Island, off the Danco Coast, Graham Land. Foyn Harbor, which lies south of the Islands, was used by whalers for the mooring and anchoring of factory ships during the early 20th century. North of Foyn Harbor, in Gouvernøren Bay, lies the wreck of a Norwegian Whaling Transport Vessel, which burnt and sank there in 1916, now providing a spectacular dive site.

CONDITIONS

Upon surface approach, one can see the wreck sticking partly out of the water. It is lying on its side, slightly askew, on an uneven rocky bottom, which slopes upward creating a gully separating the ship and shore. The gully slope is a good reference, and an interesting line to follow to the surface after the wreck has been inspected; it also takes the diver away from the tangled metal of the ship.

Take care to enter the water a good 5–10 m away from the wreck, swimming towards it, to avoid landing on any protruding pieces of metal, or damaging any delicate life growing on the ship.

Due to ice moving through the area, the upper parts of the wreck are sparsely populated, but as you descend towards the bottom of 17 m, the ship's position creates overhangs, and suddenly the life becomes more plentiful.

Special care should be taken when inspecting the surface of the boat, as new encrustations can be very delicate and easily disturbed.

There are no 'swim-throughs' on the boat, but divers can peer through old portholes and encrusted doors, and with some careful maneuvering, divers may be able to glimpse some of the ship's inner areas.

Depth:
17 m

Ice:
As the wreck is lying in a small bay, ice can gather around it and get trapped. This may inhibit diving the site. In most cases this ice is easy to move away, allowing an entry and exit spot to be opened.

What you might see:
Sea urchins
Sea stars
Limpets
Clams
Worms
Notothenids
Anemones
Sponges
Nudibranchs

FACING PAGE:
LEFT: Krill *Euphasia superba* (*top*); Brittle star *Ophionotus victoriae* (*bottom*)
RIGHT: Whale bones (*top*); Encrusted hull of the wreck (*bottom*).

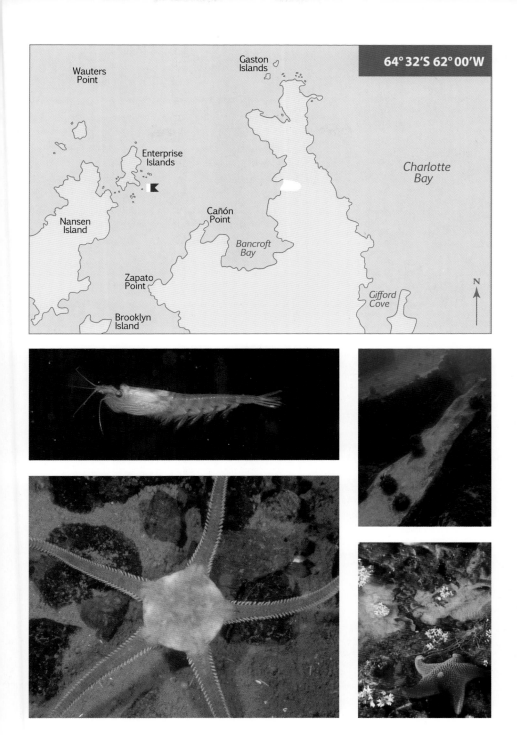

Gaston
Islands

Wauters
Point

Enterprise
Islands

Charlotte
Bay

Cañón
Point

Nansen
Island

Bancroft
Bay

Zapato
Point

Gifford
Cove

N

Brooklyn
Island

Orne Harbor is a two-kilometer-wide indentation into the west coast of Graham Land and was discovered and documented by the Belgium Antarctic Expedition under Gerlache. However, the name Orne Harbor was probably given by the Norwegian whalers, because it was used by Scottish Geologist David Ferguson on his geologic study of the area on the *Hanka* in 1913. The landing site here offers one of the few places on the continent of Antarctica where visitors can land comfortably and climb up to a fantastic lookout over the Errera Channel.

CONDITIONS

To the west of the approved landing rock, there is a sheer rock face that extends down from Spigot Peak. The entrance point for the dive is on this sheer face. Because the underwater topography mimics that above the surface, it is necessary to begin the decent almost touching the wall, lest one becomes disoriented and is not able to find it. The wall drops straight down to 27 m, before becoming a steep slope. The top 3 m are scoured by the brash ice that pours into the harbor from the many glaciers in the area. Deeper than 3 m is a garden of sponges and other invertebrates. Because of the sheer nature of the wall and small overhangs, there are huge swathes of big healthy sponges.

Depth:
Up to 40 m

Ice:
Depending on the wind direction, brash ice from the nearby glaciers can completely obscure the dive site; winds from the northeast are the most problematic.

What you might see:
TOP **5** M:
Sea stars
Limpets
Algae
Amphipods

BELOW **10** M:
Sun stars
Nudibranchs
Sponges
Brittle stars
Worms
Notothenids

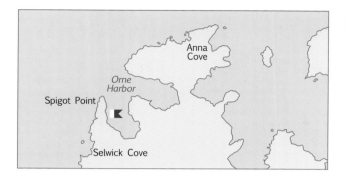

LEFT: One of the many filter-feeding anemones in Antarctica (*top*); A Giant Isopod scavenges for food (*bottom*); RIGHT: An Antarctic hydroid, a colonial animal (*top*); An Antarctic soft coral, related to the hydroid shown above (*bottom*).

FACING PAGE: Antarctic Shrimp *Chorismus antarcticus*.

Once reaching depth, it is suggested to swim from north to south (towards the landing site) until you find an obvious ravine that can be followed to the surface. The ravine, bordered by the wall on the north side and a steep slope on the south side, holds many photographic opportunities of other invertebrates found in and amongst the ravine debris.

Cuverville is a rocky, towering island lying in the Errera Channel between the Arctowski peninsula and the northern part of Rongé Island. It was discovered by the ship *Belgica* under Gerlache, who named it for J.M.A. Cavelier de Cuverville, a vice admiral of the French Navy.

Often visited, and home to several large Gentoo Penguin colonies, it was the site of a University of Cambridge study (1992–95) to try and determine the effects of tourism on penguins. After physiological and observational monitoring, the conclusion that was drawn was that well-managed tour groups, who followed *Visitor Guidelines to Antarctica*, had no detrimental consequence on the penguin's breeding.

Depth:
Up to 40 m

Ice:
This area can be clogged with ice, and larger icebergs grounded within the bay area, as well as outside, making diving impossible, but in most cases at least one of the sites is open

What you might see:
SCOUR ZONE:
Limpets
Algae
Sea stars
Sea urchins
Gentoo Penguins
   swimming

DEEPER DIVES:
Sea urchins
Sea stars
Sheets of algae
Sponges
Anemones
Sea spiders

Special Note: With the existence of the Gentoo Penguin colonies on the island as well as the high prevalence of ice in the area, Leopard seals are almost always found here. These animals have become extremely habituated to Zodiacs and divers.

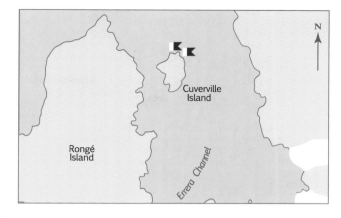

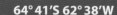

BELOW:
Antarctic Limpet *Nacella concinna* (*top*);
Anemone *Hormathia lacunifera* (*middle*); Gentoo Penguins *Pygoscelis papua* 'flying' through the shallows (*bottom*).

FACING PAGE: Notothenid.

CONDITIONS

INSIDE THE COVE

This dive site falls into the scour zone category. There are always large icebergs moving through the area, repeatedly stripping the bottom of life throughout the season. It is this small to medium sized rocky base that is home to some of the more resilient animals in Antarctica, such as worms and limpets. A major draw to diving here is the Gentoo Penguin traffic. This bay is the main water entrance and exit point for the Gentoos that inhabit the island, creating an excellent opportunity to observe or film these penguins flying underwater. It is possible to continue the dive out of the harbor and into deeper water, but for the purpose of filming or observing penguins it is suggested divers stay shallow.

WALL DIVE

This site is found on the outer edge of the eastern shore. Due to the many icebergs that transit the Errera Channel, the top 9 m is scoured. However, below 10 m some of the larger and more impressive animals of Antarctica appear. It is important to keep in mind that this site, like Paradise Harbor (*page 88*), has a lot of delicate algae and marine snow collecting on the benthic organisms, so careful body position and fining is a must to avoid disturbing the natural environment. A depth of 40 m can be reached during this dive, but 24 m is sufficient to explore the larger benthic life.

Neko Harbor is a small bay indenting the east shore of Andvord Bay and was discovered and roughly charted by Belgian explorer Adrien de Gerlache during his 1897–99 expedition. It was named for a Norwegian whaling boat, the *Neko*, which operated in the area between 1911 and 1924. The Scottish Geologist David Ferguson officially published the name in 1921.

CONDITIONS

To the southeast of the approved landing beach is a small rocky outcropping that extends approximately 8 m from the ice wall. In this particular area the ice cliff is a shallow slope, representing a relatively safe and non-active area, giving shelter from any possible calving events. Upon dropping into the water, divers find themselves on a gradual slope. The upper 15 m are very scoured by the large icebergs that move through the area, and it is not unusual to find scour trenches at 24 m. Because of the constant ice movement, the dynamics of this dive site change all the time, and one never knows what will be found from week to week, or even day to day. To find the most delicate of invertebrates, look for the large glacial erratic (rocks dropped by the large icebergs), where these creatures can find a stable and safe environment on which to live.

Special Note: After the dive, with good visibility, it is often possible to snorkel close by the landing site that is often the entry and exit point for the nesting Gentoo Penguins, and take some memorable photos.

Depth:

Up to 40 m

Ice:

Depending on the tide and wind direction, the dive site may be obscured by ice. Wind blowing from the southeast will cause the most problems. Regardless of brash ice, there are often bergy bits and brash ice floating in the water, so be sure to be aware of your surroundings as you ascend.

What you might see:

TOP **5 M:**
Sea stars
Limpets
Algae
Amphipods

BELOW **15 M:**
Sun stars
Nudibranchs
Sponges
Tunicates
Worms
Sea stars

Possible Secondary Dive Site

Approximately two kilometers across Andvord Bay to the southeast lies Forbes Point. At the time of publication, this site has not been dived but has good potential. Forbes Point is a sheer rock wall, with no hanging glacier, extending straight down to the water. The charted water depths surrounding this point are very deep, suggesting a nice wall beneath the surface. Beware of ice conditions before you start off for this dive site as wind blowing from the northwest will most likely push ice into the dive site and obscure it.

Andvord Bay

Neko Harbor

Forbes Point

Lester Cove

LEFT: Antarctic Sun Star *Labidiaster radiosus* (*top*); *Perknaster aurorae* – a sponge eater (*bottom*); RIGHT: An amphipod rests on a sponge (*top*); Two of the gastropod species of the Antarctic (*bottom*).

Paradise Harbor is a wide embayment behind Lemaire and Byrde Islands, indenting the Danco coast of Graham Land. It was used and named by whalers in the 1920s, later becoming the site of the Argentine Station, Almirante Brown, and Chilean Station, González Videla. This dive site is named after the breeding colony of Antarctic Shags on the cliffs above.

CONDITIONS

Directly below the nesting shags, is one of the most spectacular wall dives in the Antarctic, which drops straight down to 75 m. The top 3 m of the wall are generally scoured by ice, the richest life found below 18 m. I suggest descending directly below the first group of shag nests, and move slowly along the wall toward the east, keeping it on your left shoulder. There can be a current running along the wall, but is generally negligible.

Due to the richness of the wall and water (partly thanks to the shags above) there is always a lot of marine snow on the benthic animals, as well as a delicate algae that lines the wall. Both are easily disturbed, and therefore attention to body position and fining are required.

Depth:
Up to 40 m

Ice:
The wall is generally ice free, except for possible bergy bits or brash ice floating on the surface, but these are easily avoided and worked around.

What you might see:
TOP **7** M:
Limpets
Algae
Amphipods
Worms

BELOW **7** M:
Sponges
Anemones
Notothenids
Shrimp
Chitin
Sea spiders
Tunicates
Nudibranchs
Worms

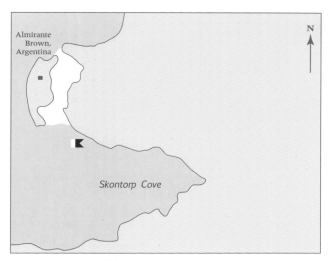

LEFT: Terrebellid worm (*top*); Limpets and algae are predominant species on the upper wall of Paradise Harbor (*bottom*); RIGHT: The protected nature of 'The Shag Wall' makes it a safe haven for a plethora of species (*top*); Antarctic Shag *Phalacrocorax bransfieldensis* nests mark the dive site (*bottom*).

FACING PAGE: Giant Isopod *Glyptonotus arcticus*.

Almirante Brown, Argentina

Skontorp Cove

Port Lockroy, an 800 m-long harbor on Weincke Island's west coast, was a major haven for whalers until 1930. In 1943, it became the site of British Research Base A, where scientists focused their studies on meteorology. The permanent base home, Bransfield House, was built in February 1944 on Goudier Island, and staffed almost continuously until 1962.

Between January and March 1996 the hut was restored and listed as a Historic Site. Now, each summer it is manned and operated by the UK Antarctic Heritage Trust. It is the most visited site in Antarctica.

CONDITIONS

OFF BRANSFIELD HOUSE, GOUDIER ISLAND

Early in the season the area around both Goudier and Wienke Islands is often covered by fast ice, which makes diving between the two impossible. If this is the case, a dive can usually be made off the passenger landing spot on Goudier.

Depth:
11–18 m

Ice:
Ice may obscure the preferred dive site. Additionally large bergy bits, as well as brash ice from the glacier may be present at any time of the year.

What you might see:
Green algae
Limpets
Whale bones
Worms
Sea stars
Anemones
Sponges
Small isopods
Giant Isopods
Notothenids
Leopard Seal
Weddell Seal

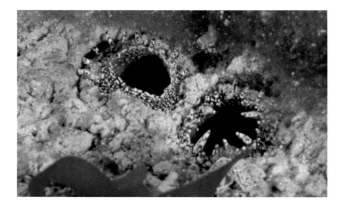

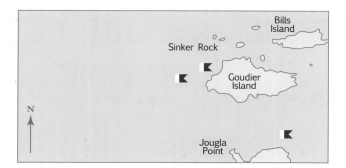

Top: Whale bones line the bottom of Port Lockroy; Bottom: A pair of Giant Isopods *Glyptonotus arcticus.*

Facing page: Soft Shell Clam (*above*); Notothenid (*below*).

However, keep in mind that the seabed in this area drops off quickly going from 4–18 m in a very short distance, and continues to almost 62 m further out in the harbor. The rocky bottom is covered in soft algae which tears easily, so it is important that meticulous fining is used. There are whale bones strewn over the bottom, but as these are covered with marine snow, it is important to minimizing diving movements to reduce the risk of visibility being disrupted.

BETWEEN GOUDIER AND JOUGLA POINT, WIENCKE ISLAND

This is the preferred dive site at Port Lockroy, but brash ice and bergy bits may impinge at any time of the year, causing entry and exit to be precarious. The bottom at this site slopes gradually from 6 m, stopping at 19 m. The top 3 m of the water column are generally pretty murky whatever the time of year, especially with boat traffic disturbing the bottom. But early in the season, upon reaching 10 m, the silt stops and the bottom can suddenly open up in front of you – as if a thermacline has separated layers of two different water temperatures. At this point visibility could be 12–20 m, giving you a spectacular look at the whale bones strewn across the bottom. However, later in the season the visibility completely clouds, and the deeper a diver goes, the darker it gets, so flashlights and high-powered strobes are good pieces of equipment to have. Although not covered in soft algae, the sea floor is similar to that around both Goudier and Wienke Islands, as it is covered with a fine marine snow that is easily disturbed. Whale bones continue to be scattered on the bottom, and partial and full skeletons may be visible.

ABOVE: Diver behind a piece of the *Bahia Paraiso*;
RIGHT: Tunicate;
BELOW: Polychete worm *Potamilla antarctica*.

Depth:
20 m

Ice:
Generally not present at dive site, except for a small amount of brash ice from the inner glacier. However, getting to the dive site can still be hazardous.

Oil:
A small slick can still be seen spreading from the hull.

What you might see:
ON THE UPPER AND OUTER METAL:
Sea stars
Limpets
Algae

ON THE UNDERSIDE OF THE SHIP:
Encrusting sponges
Tunicates
Sessile jellyfish
Worms

Special Note: Arthur Harbor is notorious for its resident Leopard Seals. They are very accustomed to humans, Zodiacs, and divers, and may be troublesome during a dive.
Be sure to ask permission to dive the *Bahia Paraiso* from the Station Manager at Palmer.

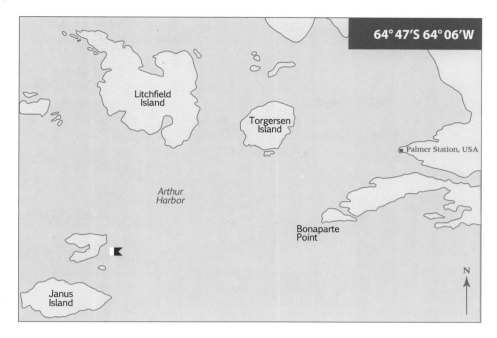

64° 47'S 64° 06'W

Litchfield Island

Torgersen Island

Palmer Station, USA

Arthur Harbor

Bonaparte Point

Janus Island

N

Janus Island lies off the southwest coast of Anvers Island in the Palmer Archipelago, named for US sealer and explorer Nathaniel B. Palmer. The island is the southernmost on the west side of the entrance to Arthur Harbor, and it is between here and De Laca Island that the wreck of the *Bahia Paraiso* lies. The US Antarctic Program's Palmer Station is located on Anvers Island, on the eastern side of Arthur Harbor.

The 134 m Argentine research supply vessel *Bahia Paraiso* went aground in Arthur Harbor in 1989. It ran into a submerged reef off DeLaca Island, ripping a 10 m gash in the hull, and spilling 645,000 liters of diesel fuel, creating a slick that covered 30 square kilometers and caused Antarctica's worst environmental disaster to date. All 316 people, including 82 tourists, were rescued. The ship now lies nearly submerged with only a small section of the hull visible.

CONDITIONS

From Palmer Station, it is about a 15-minute Zodiac ride out to the dive site. This ride can be very choppy and also impeded by brash ice that often fills Arthur Harbor. The wreck is visible from the surface, and the hull and one stabilizer housing can be seen upon approach.

BELOW: Sponge growth on the hanging scrap metal (*top*); Engine room of the *Bahia Paraiso* (*bottom*).

The *Bahia Paraiso* is lying capsized in 18 m of water, her bow pointing northwest. It is suggested that divers drop at least 6 m away from the hull. Although negligible current has been experienced at the site, there is almost always surge, which can knock a diver into the ship if too close.

The dive can start on either side of the wreck, but the northwest side closest to De Laca Island is recommended. It is on this side of the ship that divers can gain access to the protected under-section where some of the richest marine life is found. The outer parts of the wreck are more sparsely covered, as they are subjected to water and ice movement. At the stern of the ship the propeller looks brand new, and there are often fish here. A diver can poke into small openings and portholes, but there are no 'swim-throughs' on the *Bahia*. Bring a flashlight for looking into windows and other dark places.

A word of caution: there are stray pieces of metal hanging from the wreck, and on the bottom surrounding it. Take care to keep track of extra hoses, and equipment, as they can become entangled in the debris.

Upon ascending, be careful of surge, as it can cause a rise and fall of 1–2 m, disrupting safety stops. Staying 3–5 m away from the hull will decrease the effects.

BELOW: The port side stabilizer housing of the *Bahia Paraiso* is visible above the surface. Torgersen Island can be seen in the background.

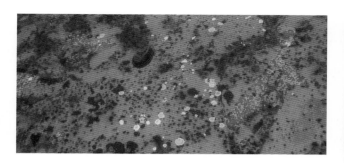

ABOVE: Rusty hull of the *Bahia Paraiso*;
BELOW: Encrusting hull of the *Bahia Paraiso* (*top*);
Sea star *Cuentoaster involutus*, on wreck debris (*bottom*)
RIGHT: Sessile jellyfish (*top*); Sea star *Diplasterias brucei* (*bottom*).

Booth Island is separated from the mainland of the Antarctic Peninsula by the famous Lemaire Channel. One of the narrowest and most scenic passages in Antarctica, the Lemaire was first navigated and charted by the Belgian Antarctic Expedition of 1895–98. Booth Island, also part of the Wilhelm Archipelago, was discovered in 1873–74 by a German sealing and whaling expedition, and makes the western wall of the channel. In 1903, Charcot wintered his ship, the *Français*, in the small bay on the north coast of the island, now named Port Charcot.

Depth:
Up to 40 m

Ice:
Early in the season there can be fast ice attached to the shore. Large icebergs often become grounded between Booth and Pléneau Islands. The natural calving of these bergs produces large quantities of bergy bits and brash ice which can disrupt boating and diving activities.

What you might see:
TOP **10** M:
Limpets
Algae
Ctenophores
Pteropods
Worms

BELOW **10** M:
Worms
Sea urchins
Anemones
Sun star
Sea stars
Tunicates
Sea cucumbers
Sponges
Nudibranchs
Notothenids
Octopus

CONDITIONS

Due to a steeply sloping shore, this is one of the deeper dives on the peninsula, easily reaching recreational dive limits. Despite being quite steep, this slope makes a good reference point for divers upon entry and exit.

The bottom here is often scoured by large icebergs that consistently move through the area, but large boulders that litter the bottom create protected refuges for benthic organisms.

A special word of caution about the icebergs found in this area: they can be very unstable. A good rule of thumb is to keep a distance of least twice the iceberg's height above the water, so in the event of a calving or roll-over, the diver is out of harm's way.

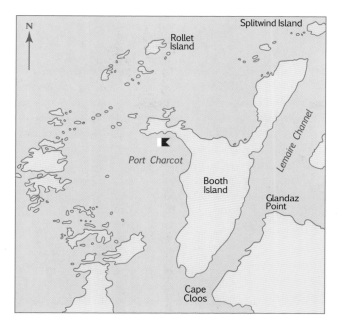

TOP: Sun star *Labidiaster radiosus*;
BOTTOM: Amenone *Isotella antarctica*.

FACING PAGE: One of the two species of octopus that inhabit the Antarctic.

Pléneau Island is located in the Wilhelm Archipelago, and was initially discovered by the German Whaling and Sealing expedition of 1873–74. In 1903–05 it was charted incorrectly as a peninsula of neighboring Hovgaard Island by Charcot, who named it for Paul Pléneau, his expedition photographer.

CONDITIONS

Pléneau's shore falls away as a pebbly slope, plateauing at 18 m on the eastern side of the island, before falling away even further. This is a grounding area for large icebergs, and is often scoured. However, there are a few boulders and protected areas where richer benthic life can be found, but in general it is a sparsely populated seabed.

A major attraction to this site is the possibility of spotting Gentoo Penguins flying through the water. Of all the penguin species, the Gentoo is the least bothered by divers, and will often come close to divers to briefly investigate. This is a great opportunity for photographers, but due to the speed at which this penguin can travel, a lot of shooting has to be done 'from the hip'. The best technique is to stay in one spot while the penguins become used to the diver's presence. This may be a cold wait, but the rewards are worth it!

On Pléneau, Weddell Seals traditionally haul out on the rocks and snow covered beaches. These seals also bask in the relatively shallow shore water of 1–5 m, and when approached carefully, are willing observation subjects.

This is a place where Leopard Seals have become habituated to boats, people, and divers, and have reportedly bitten Zodiacs. Keep a close look out. A good warning system to use here is penguin behavior; if you see the penguins swimming one way and quickly reversing direction, take a careful glance at what they were swimming away from.

Depth:
5–18 m

Ice:
Due to the grounded icebergs around the island, you can almost always count on bergy bits floating near the dive sites. However, the dive is not usually impeded by this ice.

What you might see:
Anemones
Sea stars
Ctenphores
Sea urchins
Notothenids
Gentoo Penguins
  swimming
Weddell Seals

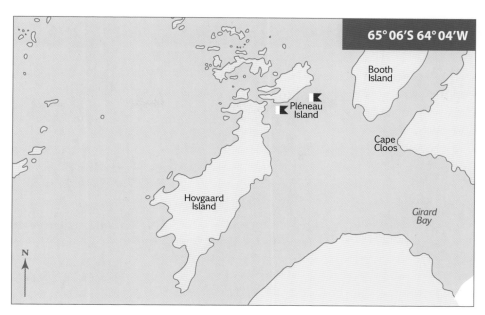

Booth Island

Pléneau Island

Cape Cloos

Hovgaard Island

Girard Bay

N

LEFT: Weddell Seal *Leptonychotes wedellii* (*top*); Gentoo Penguin *Pygoscelis papua* (*bottom*); ABOVE: Hydroid; BELOW: Amphipod *Jassa ingens*;

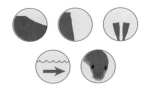

Petermann Island is located in the Wilhelm Archipelago, which was discovered by a German sealing and whaling expedition in 1873–74. It was named for August Petermann, a German geographer. During the French Antarctic Expedition of 1908–10, Charcot's ship *Porquoi Pas* found a safe over-winter mooring here, within a naturally protected harbor. Today this refuge is referred to as Port Circumcision as it was spotted on 1 January 1909, the traditional day for the Feast of the Circumcision.

In addition to colonies of Antarctic Shags and Adelie Penguins, Petermann Island is home to the southernmost Gentoo Penguin colony in the world.

Depth:
INSIDE: 7 m
OUTSIDE: Up to 40 m

Ice:
Early in the season there can be fast ice attached to shore, closing off both dive sites. Larger icebergs often lodge themselves close to Petermann's shore, and there are often bergy bits floating on the surface all around the island and within Port Circumcision.

What you might see:
PORT CIRCUMCISION:
Algae
Limpets
Sea stars
Gentoo Penguins
   swimming

ON THE EASTERN SIDE:
Sea stars
Limpets
Anemones
Sea cucumbers
Sponges
Sea spiders
Tunicates
Crinoids
Hydroids

CONDITIONS
WITHIN PORT CIRCUMCISION

This site is a safe and relatively easy dive, as inside the sheltered harbor there is negligible current or surge. The bottom is unusually shaped and undulates, rising quickly to as shallow as 1 m before dropping off again, the deepest depth being 7 m. With these rocky risks lying so close to the surface, it is important to make sure that the support boats are aware of their location in order to avoid damage.

The current along the outside of the island can cause ice to shift rapidly, closing and opening the entrance to Port Circumcision at an astounding rate. It is important to be aware of this risk if you decide to dive when there is a lot of ice in the area.

There is the possibility of finding artifacts from Charcot's expedition on the bottom of Port Circumcision, as it has been said the crew threw a good deal overboard during their over-winter stay. As with all historical items in Antarctica, please admire but leave them for others to enjoy.

Special Note: This is a fantastic area to view Humpback, Killer, and Minke whales later in the season (late December through February). The animals are often moving and feeding, so a Splash Cam may be the best way to get an underwater view. Be sure to pay attention to the *Marine Wildlife Watching Guidelines (page 126)*. Take care not to dive too close to the icebergs that lodge close to the shore, as they are often unstable and could shift position at any time, possibly trapping a diver.

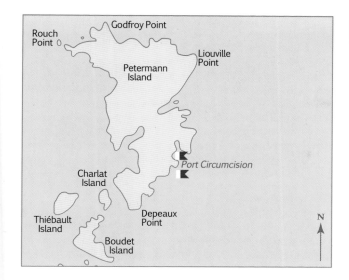

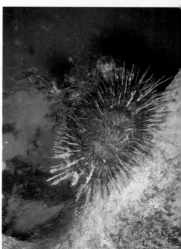

Top: Nudibranch
Austrodoris kerguelensis;
Bottom: Sea urchin
Sterechinus neumayeri.

On the eastern side

The shore of Petermann Island slopes down steeply, resulting in a dramatic wall dive. There can be a strong tidal current outside the shelter of Port Circumcision, so it is suggested that dives be made as close to slack water as possible. The combination of strong current and a steeply sloping bottom makes it easy to become disorientated. As with the Aitcho Islands (*page 70*), it easy to get swept away from the dive site and out into open water.

The current can also cause ice to shift, blocking the entrance and exit point to the dive. Make sure that the surface support keeps a sharp eye on current and ice conditions, and that a diver recall system is in place.

The dive begins on a shelving wall that is quite scoured by ice for the first 8 m, but does give you a look at the resilient animals such as urchins and limpets. The wall continues down to 40 m where it hits another wider shelf before continuing to extreme depths. At depths of 15–40 m is where many of the delicate filter feeders, such as anemones and hydroids, live.

Prospect Point is located on the west coast of Graham Land, east of the Fish Islands. It was the site of British Research Base J, built in 1957 and occupied for geological and survey work until 1959. The hut was dismantled in June 2004.

CONDITIONS

This area is frequently scoured by large ice floes that drift north from below the Antarctic Circle. It is because of this ice scour that areas around the old hut site, as well as other rocky coves, offer little as dive sites.

The preferred dive site is the wall on the southern side of Perch Island, which drops dramatically to 60 m. There can be a strong tidal current running along this wall, which can not only disrupt dive practices, but can also move ice into the exit point. For these reasons, it is suggested that dives be made as close to slack water as possible.

Depth:
Up to 40 m

Ice:
Due to breakup of sea ice below the Antarctic Circle later in the season, ice can completely close off the suggested dive site. Be careful of the tidal current: although the area might be ice-free at the start of the dive, during the dive ice can flow in, inhibiting exit.
Do not dive near the very active and dangerous glaciers in the area.

What you might see:
Sea spiders
Tunicates
Limpets
Anemones
Notothenids
Sea cucumbers

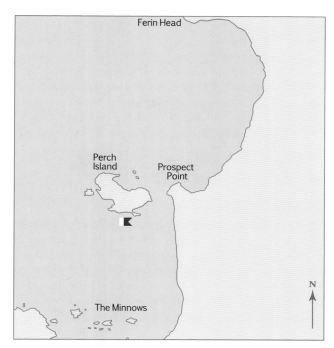

Top: Notothenids rest on rocky ledges; Bottom: Sea spider *Decalopoda australis.*

Facing page: Undescribed anemone on the Prospect wall.

Détaille Island was a British Research Base in Lallemand Fjord, Loubret Coast, Graham Land. It was discovered in 1908–10 by Charcot, who named it after Monsieur Détaille of Punta Arenas in Chile, a shareholder in Magellan Whaling Company The British Research Base was established in February 1956, and operated for three years for local survey, geological, and meteorological studies, finally closing in March 1959. The remaining hut was removed in 2006.

CONDITIONS

Although there are several sites around the island that can be dived, due to surprisingly shallow areas in what would appear to be deep water, a careful study of the depths on a nautical chart is recommended.

The dives here are all wall dives or very steep rock slopes. Due to ice flowing north from the Antarctic Circle, the walls can be scoured, especially above 5 m. However, there are small ledges, at varying intervals, that offer a resting place or secure spot for animals to attach.

The tidal current moves quickly here, and can sweep a diver around the island corners, away from the support boat. It is important to inform the surface of this, allowing them to take into account all factors to safely retrieve the diver.

Depth:
8–20 m

Ice:
This area lies exposed and therefore is scoured by large icebergs coming up from below the circle. There are also bergy bits floating all around the island, which can infringe upon the dive sites. Luckily there is more than one dive site to choose from.

What you might see:
TOP **12 M:**
Ctenophores
Limpets
Sea stars
Worms
Amphipods
Isopods

BELOW **12 M:**
Anemones
Tunicates
Encrusting sponges
Notothenids

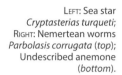

LEFT: Sea star
Cryptasterias turqueti;
RIGHT: Nemertean worms
Parbolasis corrugata (top);
Undescribed anemone
(bottom).

FACING PAGE:
Isopod *Serolis corunta.*

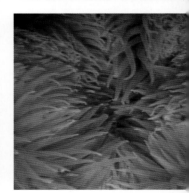

Stonington is an island off the Falliéres Coast of Southern Graham Land. Named for the whaling port of Stonington, Connecticut, USA, home to the sloop *Hero* in which Captain Nathanial B. Palmer sighted the Antarctic continent in 1820, it was selected by the US Antarctic Service Expedition of 1939–41 as the site for their east station, being an ideal spot to gain direct access to the Graham Land Plateau.

In 1945–46 it became the site of British Base E, originally run by the Falkland Islands Dependencies Survey until February 1950. Due to a fire, a new two-storey hut was built in March 1961 and occupied until February 1975. The hut remains, and is now a historic monument, although infrequently visited by tourists.

CONDITIONS
Directly off the landing site, near the huts on Stonington Island, there is a rocky mound. This can easily be identified on marine charts, and can be seen from the surface even in moderate visibility; divers often stand on it while taking off their gear at the end of the dive. This rocky mound drops off to 21 m, stopping on a bottom that looks somewhat barren at first glance, but on closer investigation the large cracks in the rock bed create ideal locations for creatures to take refuge.

Depth:
3–21 m

Ice:
In the early season this area is often inaccessible to non-icebreaking ships, due to fast ice and large floes. Throughout the year, a constant stream of bergy bits and brash ice come through the area, and can block the dive site.

What you might see:
Limpets
Sea urchins
Anemones
Encrusting sponges
Tunicates
Scallops
Weddell Seal

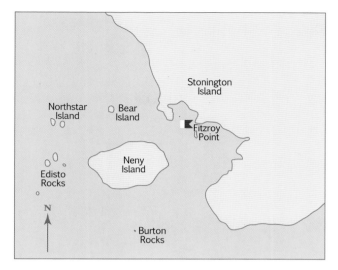

LEFT: Protected crevices provide shelter for a variety of species; RIGHT: Tunicate *Cnemidocarpa verrucosa* (*top*); Small bivalves line cracks in the rock bed (*bottom*).

FACING PAGE: Sea star stomach.

107

Above: Giant Isopod *Glyptonotus arcticus*; Below: Sea spider *Pallenopsis notiosa*.

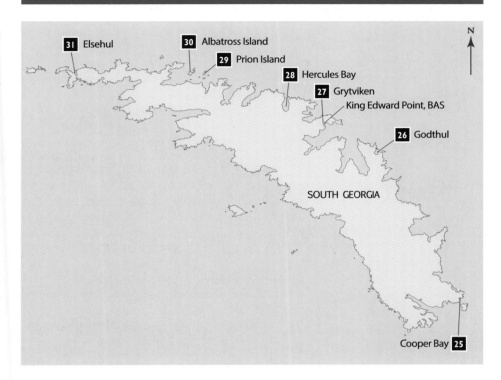

Diving in South Georgia

South Georgia is an island 170 km long that lies to the northeast of the Antarctic Peninsula, and southeast of the Falkland Islands. Upon approach from the sea, it is a striking land mass diversified by towering snow-capped mountains, lush, glacially carved valleys of green low-lying vegetation, and rushing melt-water streams.

The island was charted, named, and claimed for Britain by Captain James Cook in 1775. Throughout history, it has most notably been home to several international sealing and whaling companies, and in recent times a site of combat during the Falkland Islands War.

Although not part of Antarctica, South Georgia is a frequently visited sub-Antarctic island, and is often included in expedition trips to the Antarctic Peninsula.

The diving on South Georgia is more rich and diverse than on the Antarctic Peninsula, and one of the most southerly kelp forests on the planet can be found here. Due to this abundance of undersea flora and fauna, there are a few special considerations to take into account when diving around South Georgia.

VISIBILITY

Visibility disruption in South Georgia is not as strongly linked to the seasonal plankton bloom as it is on the Antarctic Peninsula. There is a plankton bloom, but most of the time marine snow and glacial flower are the main culprits of low visibility. Due to large kelp plants, their inhabiting amphipods and isopods, as well as the large numbers of bird colonies found on and around South Georgia, there is a lot of marine snow in the water column, which tends to collect on kelp fronds. When the fronds are disturbed, by swell or divers, the marine snow shaken off the frond or stirred from the bottom, enters the water column. This can hamper visibility as much, or more than, plankton blooms do around the Peninsula. Glacial flower is an added problem, as many dive sites are near glaciers or in the path of their runoff. When the tide is moving in the right direction, the current can take the glacial flower into a dive site, creating a zero-visibility environment.

KELP

Kelp, especially with surge, can wreak havoc to a diver and his or her equipment by entanglement. To reduce this risk, make sure all gauges are tucked closely to the body, carry a knife on your hose rather than your leg for easier access, and always have a buddy close by to help you out if you become entangled. The key thing to remember if this does happen is to remain calm and not to thrash. Stop, figure out where the problem is, and then work from there to release yourself.

Although the kelp can cause many difficulties for divers, it is an amazing plant, being incredibly tough and resilient, well able to withstand the rough seas of the Southern Ocean.

However, kelp is not only a plant in its own right but also forms dense forests within which communities of many underwater animals of live. While diving around the kelp of South Georgia, be sure to lift the fronds that lie on the bottom, look carefully into the holdfasts, and check out what is in and on the fronds.

FUR SEALS

In most diveable areas, the beaches and kelp are swarming with Antarctic Fur Seals, above and below the water. Fur seals behave similarly to sea lions and are inquisitive about divers. They often swim at high speeds past divers and will nip, making light contact, but nothing injury-worthy unless striking bare skin. The seals are curious about bubbles, but do not blow bubbles themselves; and while they have not been observed to take regulator hoses, it is worth bearing in mind that this is a possibility.

As a general rule, where there is one fur seal there will be many more, and shortly after the first becomes inquisitive, it is not long before its friends and relatives follow, creating an environment where the diver can be surrounded by up to 30 seals at a time.

The adult male fur seals can be very territorial, especially in the breeding season during October and November. It is a good habit to be wary of them at this time, both in and out of the water, as they have been known to attack humans on land.

ICE

Ice is generally not a problem for divers around South Georgia.

Cooper Bay indents the southeastern end of South Georgia, its name derived from nearby Cooper Island, a rat-free island which is not allowed to be visited by tourists.

CONDITIONS

This bay has many available dive sites depending on the conditions. On almost all occasions one can find a sheltered spot to launch dive operations, despite bad weather in other localities.

The most attractive dive sites here are kelp forest, where the plant not only attaches to the bottom but also flows across it. The dive sites are generally exposed to swell and weather coming in from the south, and although it may be calm and sunny on the surface, there is often surge moving horizontally across the bottom, making it difficult for a diver to stay in one spot. Moreover, the surge dissipates the marine snow, which can lower visibility.

It can take some work to view the benthic creatures that inhabit Cooper Bay. They often take refuge underneath the kelp or stay hidden under rocky ledges, so be sure to take a close look.

Later in the season (February and March) is one of the most active times for fur seal pups and juveniles, and you are liable to find great numbers swimming around you.

Depth:
12–21 m

Ice:
Ice is generally not a problem in Cooper Bay. However, large icebergs sometimes ground on the outside of Cooper Sound, which can create small bergy bits, but this has never impeded diving.

What you might see:
Kelp
Limpets
Amphipods
Isopods
Anemones
Notothenids
Hydroids
Fur seals
Giant Isopods
Sea spiders
Sponges
Ascidians
Sessile jellyfish
Chinstrap or Gentoo
  Penguins swimming

IN THE WATER COLUMN:
Ctenophores
Pteropods
Hydroids

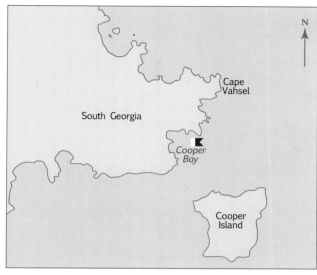

Left: Antarctic Limpet
Nacella concinna (*top*);
Anemone (*bottom*);
Right: Siphonophore.

Facing page:
Notothenid *Harpagifer* sp.

Godthul is the site of the only floating whale factory accompanied by a shore base on South Georgia. On 16 September 1908 a Norwegian company purchased the South Georgia Exploration Company's lease and was granted a whaling license. The site was used from 1908/09 to 1916/17, and again from 1922/23 to 1928/29, after which the lease lapsed and the site reverted back to the British government. The inside of the bay offers a combination of both wall and kelp forest settings.

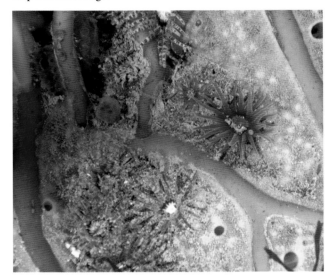

Depth:
Up to 40 m

What you might see:
Giant Kelp
Ctenophores
Sea stars
Brittle stars
Limpets
Anemones
Tunicates
Sea spiders
Nudibranchs
Fur seals (possibly)

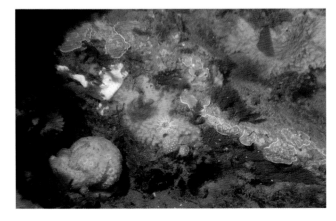

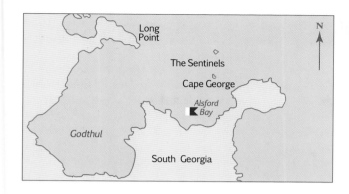

Top: Ascidian *Sycozoa sigillinoides*; Middle: Ascidians on kelp fronds; Bottom: Nudibranch *Eubranchus* sp.

Facing page: Undescribed anemone (*top*); Encrusted portion of the Godthul wall (*bottom*).

CONDITIONS

Wall Dive

Off the second promontory in Alsford Bay, there is a fantastic wall dive. From the surface the wall is not entirely obvious as it starts from a buttress found 12 m below. The top of this buttress is also thickly overgrown with kelp, which can lead to confusion as to where the entry point is, as it looks so similar to the surrounding kelp forest. It is therefore important to count the promontories as you are looking east into the bay. This wall dive continues well beyond recreational diving, and exhibits brightly colored nudibranchs and sea spiders. If a diver happens to miss the wall, all is not lost, as on either side of this buttress there are steep slopes lined with kelp, as described below.

Kelp Forest Dive

To access the kelp forest it is suggested that a diver find a point midway between the shore and the edge of the kelp to enter the water. Follow the kelp to the bottom, and once there a fantastic habitat of small and large creatures comes into view. What makes the kelp forest in Godthul so unique is that the kelp also flows down the slopes, covering the rocky seabed. Be sure to lift up the giant fronds and see what is underneath; there have been three different types of sea spiders noted here, as well as delicate hydroids, and anemones.

Grytviken, the oldest of the whaling stations on South Georgia, was founded by Captain Carl Anton Larsen in 1904. Although probably most famous for the grave of Sir Ernest Shackleton, who is buried in Grytiviken cemetery, in more recent history, Grytviken was the site of several battles during the 1982 Falkland Islands War. Legacy of this war can be found on the hill about a mile away from the cemetery, in the form of a wrecked Puma helicopter.

In recent years, Grytviken has undergone, and continues to partake in, a massive clean-up: asbestos and other hazardous materials have been removed, and the sunken whaling ships re-floated. This has made the area safe and enjoyable for visitors to walk through, allowing them to further enjoy the history of South Georgia.

A British Antarctic Survey (BAS) Research Base is located on King Edward Point (KEP), just east of the historic whaling station.

CONDITIONS

MAN-MADE STRUCTURES

The dock at KEP provides a protected dive site, and a relatively stable platform on which benthos thrives. Strange hydroids and anemones find a static structure to attach to, and even in relatively shallow depths of 4 m, life abounds. However, this is an area of high boat traffic, as well as a working pier, so be sure to coordinate with the base commander before initiating a dive.

PIER AT GRYTVIKEN

As massive construction at Grytviken has stopped, it is once again possible to dive the newly constructed and original piers of Grytviken whaling station. These piers provide a protected site for creatures to grow and flourish. Attached to the pilings you will find small mollusks as well as hydroids. Sponges are

Depth:
4–18 m

What you might see:
Kelp
Sea stars
Brittle stars
Limpets
Amphipods
Hydroids
Anemones
Tunicates
Sea spiders

Special Note: As Grytviken was a site of major conflict during the Falklands War, it is possible that a diver might come across an unexploded ordinance. If this happens, DO NOT touch the ordinance, abort the dive, estimate your position, and report the sighting to the marine office at King Edward Point as soon as possible.

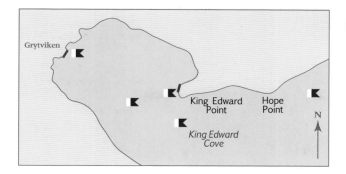

Below: Sea star *Diplasterias brucei* amongst brittle stars *Ophionotus victoriae* (*top*); Hydroid *Tubularia* sp. (*bottom*).

Left: Re-floated whalers in Grytviken Harbor (*bottom left*); Orange anemone (*bottom center*).

abundant, as are the sea spiders that feed on them. This dive is very shallow, the piers having a depth of 4 m at most, falling off into open water of 7 m. The bottom is soft so careful fining is necessary. In order to have complete control of your buoyancy I would suggest putting a few more pounds of weight into your belt. Not only will this allow you to move more efficiently, it will also allow you to put a bit of air (*i.e.* warmth) into your suit at this shallow depth. Be sure to check with the marine officer that it is OK to dive.

THE KELP FOREST

The other option for diving is the patchy kelp forest found sporadically throughout Cumberland East Bay.

It is important to note that on an incoming tide, the fine glacial flower from the nearby glaciers will enter into the bay, creating near zero visibility. On the other hand, when the tide is going out, the water can be spectacularly clear, so pay close attention to the tidal schedule.

The bottom at all dive sites is covered with a fine silt, which combined with careless fining, can create a silt storm, reducing visibility considerably. However, especially within the bay at the front of Grytviken, there are whale bones strewn across the bottom which provide attachment points for small hydroids and anemones.

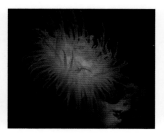

Hercules Bay is a two-kilometer-wide indentation into the north coast of South Georgia. It was named by Norwegian Whalers after the *Hercules* (or *Herkules*), a whale-catcher that frequented the bay. Above the surface it has a plethora of bird life, including Macaroni Penguins and Black-browed, Grey-headed, and Light-mantled Albatrosses.

CONDITIONS

Just about anywhere in the bay offers a phenomenal kelp dive, although the north and south sides away from the freshwater runoff will offer the best visibility and diversity of life.

All dive sites will offer similar topography, with little current. However, if there is a north or easterly swell, the dive can be surgey even at very deep depths.

As with all dives in the kelp forest, pay particular attention to the entry point, so as not to get entangled in the kelp. Divers should start outside the densest part of the kelp beds, moving further into the kelp forest after the initial descent.

As the decent and penetration into the forest continues, the bottom is reached. Here the landscape is full of nooks and crannies where invertebrates can find a protected environment. The kelp fronds are also full of life, but it is suggested to leave these for the ascent. Keep a look out for pelagics, such as ctenophores and jellyfish, as you decend and ascend.

Depth:
Up to 40 m

What you might see:
Kelp
Limpets
Amphipods
Isopods
Anemones
Notothenids
Hydroids
Giant Isopods
Sea spiders
Sponges
Ascidians

Macaroni Penguins

In the Water Column:
Hydroids
Pteropods
Ctenophores
Amphipods
Salps
Comb jellies

Hercules Bay

N

LEFT: Sea spiders generally feed on soft-bodied animals such as sponges and hydroids (*top*); Nudibranchs are able to use the defense mechanisms or toxins from their prey for their own protection (*bottom*).
RIGHT: The walls of South Georgia are home to dozens of species, most of which make use of the strong currents around the island to filter-feed (*top*); and (*bottom*).

FACING PAGE: *Astrodoris kerguelensis* – a sponge-eating nudibranch.

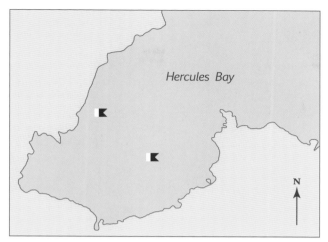

Prion and Albatross Islands lie in the Bay of Isles. They were first charted in 1912–13 by Robert Cushman Murphy, the American naturalist, and so named for the species of birds he found there: the albatrosses and prions respectively. Covered in lush moss and tussock grass, these frequently visited islands are rat-free, creating a safe nesting site for several species of ground-nesting birds, most notably the magnificent Wandering Albatross.

Special restrictions are in place to protect these delicate islands. Albatross Island is closed to visitors, and Prion Island is closed during the peak fur seal breeding season (20 November to 7 January), and at other times has a limit of 50 people on land at any one time, led in small groups by expedition staff. A boardwalk has been constructed on which visitors must remain at all times to avoid damaging the vegetation and disturbing the wildlife.

RIGHT: Antarctic Limpet *Nacella concinna* (*top*); Ascidians (*bottom left*); Chitin (*bottom right*).

Depth:
23 m

What you might see:
Kelp
Limpets
Amphipods
Isopods
Anemones
Notothenids
Hydroids
Fur seals
Giant Isopods
Sea spiders
Sponges
Ascidians

IN THE WATER COLUMN:
Hydroids
Pteropods
Ctenophores
Amphipods

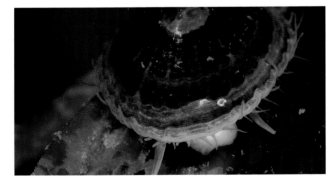

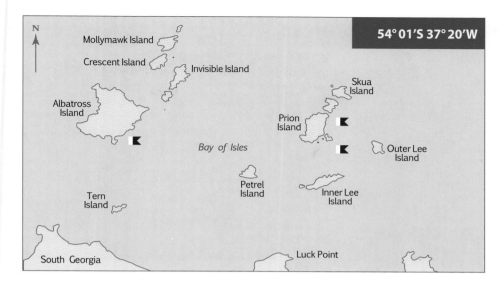

N

Mollymawk Island
Crescent Island
Invisible Island
Albatross Island
Skua Island
Prion Island
Bay of Isles
Outer Lee Island
Tern Island
Petrel Island
Inner Lee Island
South Georgia
Luck Point

54° 01'S 37° 20'W

CONDITIONS

The two islands offer similar diving conditions and topography. In both cases, the dive begins by dropping into a large area of kelp forest, where the diver follows the kelp to the bottom. The initial drop into the water can be quite tricky, as kelp is often clumped together by wind and current, which may make it difficult to find a clear spot in which to enter the water. Even after dropping into the water, any surface current can push a diver into the kelp, increasing the probability of initial entanglement, which can be time consuming and confusing from which to escape.

The descent to the bottom can be interesting, as there are often quite a few pelagic creatures and animals inhabiting the kelp, but it is suggested to save these for the ascent, as they can make interesting viewing during safety stops.

The seabed is rocky and has many nooks and crannies where small delicate creatures can take refuge. Be sure to look under rocks, fronds of kelp, and in holdfasts for interesting animals, but move slowly as some of the creatures, such as fish, will move away rapidly if startled.

There may be a surge around the islands, that generally runs horizontally, making static bottom positions difficult.

BELOW: Anemone sp *(top)*;
Antarctic Fur Seal
Arctocephalus gazella (bottom).

Elsehul is a bay, about a kilometer wide, on the northwestern extremity of South Georgia. Its name is Norwegian for Else Cove and dates back to the early 1900s when Norwegian sealers and whalers were working in this area. In the 1960s, it became a botanical study site for British Antarctic Survey scientists, and the remains of their hut can still seen on an inner beach. Elsehul supports one of the largest colonies of Macaroni Penguins on South Georgia.

CONDITIONS

The entrance to the bay is exposed to the north, and is often disturbed by weather and swell coming from that direction. For divers, the surge that results is a movement that sweeps horizontally across the seabed, rather than vertically. Although this does not cause a change in depth, it does make staying in one spot during the dive especially difficult.

All of the dive sites are in kelp forest where the bottom is found around 18 m. The kelp here not only grows up and down, but flows across the bottom in some areas, making good cover for all sorts of creatures. The rocky bottom not only provides stable anchorage points for the kelp holdfasts, but also ideal conditions for many other organisms that require a firm substrate.

Depth:
18 m

What you might see:
Sessile jellyfish
Anemones
Sea cucumbers
Limpets
Chitins
Amphipods
Isopods
Giant Isopods
Arrow worms
Copepods
Notothenids
Fur seals

NEAR THE PENGUIN COLONY:
Swimming Macaroni
  Penguins

IN THE WATER COLUMN:
Ctenophores
Pteropods
Salps
Arrow worms

Special Note: This is a fantastic area for Zodiac cruising due to the incredible wildlife all around the bay. Even if the water conditions make diving impossible, it is well worth the venture, so take advantage of the opportunity if you can.

Later in the season (February and early March), the water in Elsehul is teeming with fur seal pups. They generally stay in the upper 6 m of water column, playing within the kelp, so after a deeper dive for benthos, it can be interesting to come up into the shallows to observe the pups.

While at the edge of their range, there have been accounts of inquisitive Leopard Seals in this bay, which for several seasons in a row were observed mouthing the propellers of Zodiacs, so take the necessary precautions.

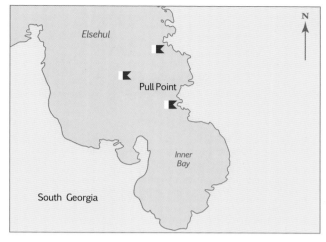

Elsehul

N

Pull Point

Inner
Bay

South Georgia

Left: Siphonophore (*top*);
Nudibranch *Cuthona* sp.
(*bottom*)
Right: Undescribed anemone
(*top*); Antarctic Fur Seal pup
Arctocephalus gazella (*bottom*)

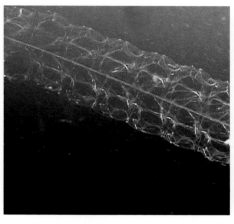

GUIDANCE FOR VISITORS TO THE ANTARCTIC

**Recommendation XVIII-1, adopted at the
Antarctic Treaty Meeting, Kyoto, 1994**

Activities in the Antarctic are governed by the Antarctic Treaty of 1959 and associated agreements, referred to collectively as the Antarctic Treaty System. The Treaty established Antarctica as a zone of peace and science.

In 1991, the Antarctic Treaty Consultative Parties adopted the Protocol on Environmental Protection to the Antarctic Treaty, which designates the Antarctic as a natural reserve. The Protocol sets out environmental principles, procedures and obligations for the comprehensive protection of the Antarctic environment, and its dependent and associated ecosystems. The Consultative Parties have agreed that, pending its entry into force, as far as possible and in accordance with their legal system, the provisions of the Protocol should be applied as appropriate.

The Environmental Protocol applies to tourism and non-governmental activities, as well as governmental activities in the Antarctic Treaty Area. It is intended to ensure that these activities, do not have adverse impacts on the Antarctic environment, or on its scientific and aesthetic values.

This Guidance for Visitors to the Antarctic is intended to ensure that all visitors are aware of, and are therefore able to comply with, the Treaty and the Protocol. Visitors are, of course, bound by national laws and regulations applicable to activities in the Antarctic.

Protect Antarctic Wildlife

Taking or harmful interference with Antarctic wildlife is prohibited except in accordance with a permit issued by a national authority.

- Do not use aircraft, vessels, small boats, or other means of transport in ways that disturb wildlife, either at sea or on land.
- Do not feed, touch, or handle birds or seals, or approach or photograph them in ways that cause them to alter their behavior. Special care is needed when animals are breeding or molting.
- Do not damage plants, for example by walking, driving, or landing on extensive moss beds or lichen-covered scree slopes.
- Do not use guns or explosives. Keep noise to the minimum to avoid frightening wildlife.
- Do not bring non-native plants or animals into the Antarctic such as live poultry, pet dogs and cats or house plants.

Respect Protected Areas

A variety of areas in the Antarctic have been afforded special protection because of their particular ecological, scientific, historic or other values. Entry into certain areas may be prohibited except in accordance with a permit issued by an appropriate national authority. Activities in and near designated Historic Sites and Monuments and certain other areas may be subject to special restrictions.

- Know the locations of areas that have been afforded special protection and any restrictions regarding entry and activities that can be carried out in and near them.

- Observe applicable restrictions.
- Do not damage, remove, or destroy Historic Sites or Monuments or any artifacts associated with them.

Respect Scientific Research

- Do not interfere with scientific research, facilities or equipment.
- Obtain permission before visiting Antarctic science and support facilities; reconfirm arrangements 24–72 hours before arrival; and comply with the rules regarding such visits.
- Do not interfere with, or remove, scientific equipment or marker posts, and do not disturb experimental study sites, field camps or supplies.

Be Safe

Be prepared for severe and changeable weather and ensure that your equipment and clothing meet Antarctic standards. Remember that the Antarctic environment is inhospitable, unpredictable, and potentially dangerous.

- Know your capabilities, the dangers posed by the Antarctic environment, and act accordingly. Plan activities with safety in mind at all times.
- Keep a safe distance from all wildlife, both on land and at sea.
- Take note of, and act on, the advice and instructions from your leaders; do not stray from your group.
- Do not walk onto glaciers or large snow fields without the proper equipment and experience; there is a real danger of falling into hidden crevasses.

- Do not expect a rescue service. Self-sufficiency is increased and risks reduced by sound planning, quality equipment, and trained personnel.
- Do not enter emergency refuges (except in emergencies). If you use equipment or food from a refuge, inform the nearest research station or national authority once the emergency is over.
- Respect any smoking restrictions, particularly around buildings, and take great care to safeguard against the danger of fire. This is a real hazard in the dry environment of Antarctica.

Keep Antarctica Pristine

Antarctica remains relatively pristine, the largest wilderness area on Earth. It has not yet been subjected to large scale human perturbations. Please keep it that way.

- Do not dispose of litter or garbage on land. Open burning is prohibited.
- Do not disturb or pollute lakes or streams. Any materials discarded at sea must be disposed of properly.
- Do not paint or engrave names or graffiti on rocks or buildings.
- Do not collect or take away biological or geological specimens or man-made artifacts as a souvenir, including rocks, bones, eggs, fossils, and parts or contents of buildings.
- Do not deface or vandalize buildings, whether occupied, abandoned, or unoccupied, or emergency refuges.

MARINE WILDLIFE WATCHING GUIDELINES

Introduction

The International Association of Antarctica Tour Operators (IAATO) has developed the following Wildlife Watching Guidelines to provide guidance to vessel operators while viewing cetaceans, seals, and birds in their marine environment. In addition, these guidelines suggest additional ways to comply with Annex II (Conservation of Antarctic Fauna and Flora) of the Protocol on Environmental Protection to the Antarctic Treaty. The guidelines do not replace any domestic governmental laws, but provide an additional code of conduct to help reduce potential disturbance to the marine environment. Some countries have guidelines or regulations stricter than these, and which may override these guidelines. Violations may be punishable by fines, imprisonment and, in extreme cases, seizure of vessel. Members/operators of IAATO should be aware that compliance with these guidelines might be insufficient to prevent violation of, and penalties resulting from, national laws and regulations. Compliance with the International Regulations for Preventing Collisions at Sea has priority over these guidelines at all times.

A. These Guidelines are Intended for:

- Use by any vessels … (*e.g.* ship, sailboat, yacht, Zodiac, kayak, *etc.*), by the officers, crew, expedition staff and visitors involved in navigating in wildlife-rich areas during viewing sessions. (Note: The use of jet-skis, surfboards or windsurfers should not occur in areas of known wildlife.)

- Providing standard operating procedures in order to minimize wildlife disturbance.
- Protecting cetaceans, seals and seabirds and ensuring a maximum high quality wildlife-watching experience by responsible observation. (Many passengers themselves are often highly concerned about the welfare of the wildlife and expect high standards of conduct by operators.)
- Avoiding harmful impacts on marine wildlife populations by ensuring that the normal patterns of daily and seasonal activity of the animals are maintained in the short and long term. Competent, careful boat handling avoids harming wildlife and leads to better wildlife watching.

B. Possible Impacts from Vessels

Possible negative impacts from vessel operations include physical injury, interference or disruption of normal behaviour, increased stress, increased underwater noise and possibly increased exposure to predators. In addition, animals could be exposed to increased levels of environmental contaminants such as oil from leaking outboard engines and discharged bilges. The recommended guidelines will help minimize the level of potential disturbance and should prevent the following from occurring:
- Displacement from important feeding areas.
- Disruption of feeding.
- Disruption of reproductive and other social behaviours.

- Changes to regular migratory pathways to avoid human interaction zones.
- Stress from interaction.
- Injury.
- Increased mortality or decreased productivity/survivorship (and therefore population decline).

C. Approaching Marine Mammals and Recommended Distances – General Principles

The animal/s should dictate all encounters. It is very important for vessel operators to be able to evaluate the animal/s'

behavioural patterns. This can be difficult in practice and a good reason to have experienced naturalists onboard. The guidelines take into account the approach towards the animals, arrival at and departure from an optimal viewing area, and recommended distances from the animals. Sometimes an animal will approach a vessel. If a marine mammal wants to interact, it may remain with the vessel. The vessel can then drift passively. If the animal is moving away from the vessel, it is choosing not to interact with or approach the vessel. Take all care to avoid collisions. This may include stopping, slowing down, and/or steering away from the animal/s. Do not chase or pursue animals.

Humpback Whale

Marine Wildlife Watching Guidelines (Whales & Dolphins, Seals and Seabirds) For Vessel & Zodiac Operations

The following principles apply to vessels in general:

1. WHALES & DOLPHINS

Cetaceans (Whales, Dolphins, Porpoises) should never be approached directly head-on. Ideally, they should be approached from slightly to the side and rear of the animal. Once travelling with the animal, travel parallel with it/them.

1a. Vessels, Officers, Crew, Expedition Staff:

- Keep a good lookout forward (and ideally on the sides and from the stern) where cetaceans may be present.
- Always give the animals the benefit of the doubt.
- Avoid sudden change in speed and direction (including putting vessel in reverse).
- Avoid loud noises, including conversation, whistling, *etc.*
- Keep radios on a low volume setting.
- Should a vessel get closer than the recommended minimum distance, withdraw at a constant, slow, no-wake speed, to at least the recommended minimum distance.
- If animals approach the vessel, put engines in neutral and do not re-engage propulsion until they are observed well clear of your vessel. If the animals remain in a local area, and if it is safe to do so, you may shut off the vessel's engine. Some whales will approach a silent, stationary vessel.

(Note: Allowing a vessel to drift within accepted recommended distances could constitute an approach.)

1b. Recommended Minimum Approach Distances:

- No intentional approach within 30 meters or 100 feet for Zodiacs, 100 meters or 300 feet for ships (150 m/500 ft. if ship over 20,000 tons. 200 m/600 ft. if 2 ships present).
- Current International Regulations:
  ARGENTINA & BRAZIL:
  100 m/300 ft. with engines on.
  50 m/150 ft. with engines off.
  SOUTH AFRICA:
  Licensed vessels only within 300 m/1,000 ft.
  No go zones *e.g.* Walker's Bay, Hermanus.
  AUSTRALIA:
  100 m/300 ft. whales
  50 m/150 ft. dolphins.
  NEW ZEALAND:
  50 m/150 ft.
  No wake within 300 m/1,000 ft. (NB 200 m/600 ft. from Sperm and baleen whales with calves.)
  USA:
  30 m/100 ft. except
  ALASKA:
  100 m/300 ft. and all Northern Right Whales 500 m/1,500 ft. (Handheld range finders may prove useful.)
  CANADA:
  100 m/300 ft.
- Helicopters or any aircraft should not approach closer than 300 m or 1,000 feet vertical distance. Helicopters are banned from over-flying cetaceans in Australian waters (minimum altitude 1,000 m/3,000 ft.). In New Zealand the minimum altitude is 150 m/500 ft. Argentina 150 m/500 ft. Alaska 500 m/1,500 ft.

- Aircraft should cease contact if the animals repeatedly dive or increase speed.

1c. Awareness of the Animals' Behavioural Patterns:

Be aware of changes in behaviour of the animal/s:

- If the cetacean is agitated or no longer interested in staying near the vessel, the following behavioural changes may be observed:
  - The animal starts to leave the area.
  - Regular changes in direction or speed of swimming.
  - Hasty dives.
  - Changes in respiration patterns.
  - Increased time spent diving compared to time spent at the surface.
  - Changes in acoustic behaviour.
  - Certain surface behaviours such as tail slapping or trumpet blows.
  - Changes in travelling direction.
  - Repetitive diving.
  - General agitation.
- Do not stay with the animal/s too long. Suggested: 15 minutes – 1 hour. If disturbance or change in behaviour occurs, retreat slowly and quietly.
- Never herd (circle), separate, scatter, or pursue a group of marine mammals, particularly mothers and young.
- If a cetacean approaches a vessel to bow-ride, vessels should not change course or speed suddenly. Do not enter a group of dolphins to encourage them to bow-ride.
- If a cetacean surfaces in the vicinity of your vessel, take all necessary precautions to avoid collisions. This may include stopping, slowing down, and/or steering away from the animal.
- Do not feed any wild animals. This includes throwing food or garbage in the water in their vicinity.
- Avoid touching or sudden movements that might startle the cetacean.

- If a cetacean comes close to shore or your boat, remain quiet.
- Playback of underwater sound of any kind should not occur. This includes recorded whale or dolphin sounds. By all means, do use hydrophones to listen to the underwater sounds (usually an engines off situation, ideal for Zodiacs rather than ships). The sounds can be listened to on headphones/mini speakers and, of course, recorded. There are a number of sites on the Internet, which offer hydrophones for sale.

1d. When the Vessel is In Sight of Whales:

Approximately 3,000 to 1,500 m/two to one mile away:

- Reduce speed to less than 10 knots.
- Post a dedicated lookout to assist the vessel operator in monitoring the location of all marine mammals 1,500 to 750 m/ one to half-a-mile away
- Reduce speed to 5 knots.

Approximately 750 m/half a mile or closer:

- Reduce speed to less than 5 knots.
- Maneuver vessel to avoid a head-on approach.
- Avoid sudden gear changes (*i.e.* into reverse).

1e. Close Approach Procedure for Vessels and/or Zodiacs:

Approximately 200 m/600 feet or closer:

- Approach at no faster than 'no-wake' speed or at idle, whichever is slower.
- Approach the animal/s from parallel to and slightly to the rear.
- Never attempt an approach head-on or from directly behind.
- Approach from behind and to one side at 4 or 8 o'clock to the whales heading 12 o'clock.
- Stay well clear of feeding baleen whales.
- Try to position your vessel downwind

of the animals to avoid engine fumes drifting over them.

- Communication between vessels and Zodiacs in multivessel approaches should be established, to coordinate viewing and to ensure that you do not disturb or harass the animals.
- Do not 'box-in' cetaceans or cut off their travel or exit routes. This is particularly important when more than one vessel is present.
- Vessels should position themselves adjacent to each other to ensure the cetaceans have large open avenues to depart through if desired.
- Beware of local geography – never trap animals between the vessel and shore. Assess the presence of obstacles such as other vessels, structures, natural features, rocks and shoreline.
- Remember: Avoid sudden or repeated changes in direction, speed or changing gears when close to marine mammals.

1f.   Close Approach Zone:

(Note: Ideally this should be no more than one vessel at a time)

Approximately 30 m/100 feet for Zodiacs; 100 m/300 feet for ships:

- When stopping to watch cetaceans, put your engines in neutral and allow the motor to idle without turning off; or allow the motor to idle for a minute or two before turning off. This prevents abrupt changes in noise that can startle the animals.
- Avoid excess engine use, gear changes, maneuvering or backing up to the animals. These produce sudden, large changes in underwater noise levels, which may startle, agitate or drive the animals away.
- Avoid the use of bow or stern lateral thrusters to maintain position. Thrusters can produce intensive cavitations (air bubble implosion) underwater.
- Be aware that whales may surface in unexpected locations.
- Breaching, tail-lobbing or flipper slapping whales may be socialising and may not be aware of boats. Keep your distance.
- Feeding humpback whales often emit sub-surface bubbles before rising to feed at the surface. Avoid these light green bubble patches.
- Emitting periodic noise may help whales know your location and avoid whale and boat collisions. For example, if your Zodiac engine is not running, occasionally tap on the engine casing with a hard object (not your radio!).
- If cetaceans approach within 30 m or 100 feet of your vessel, put engines in neutral and do not re-engage propulsion until they are observed clear of harm's way from your vessel. On rare occasions, whales have been seen to use ships as 'backscratchers', remain drifting.
- Stay quiet (turn that radio down) and restrict passenger movement in Zodiacs during close encounters.
- Enjoy the experience.

1g.   Departure Procedures:

- Move off at a slow 'no-wake' speed to the minimum distance of the close approach zone. Avoid engaging propellers within the minimum approach distance, if possible.
- Always move away from the animals to their rear (i.e. not in front of them).
- Do not chase or pursue 'departing' animals.

1h.   Swimming with Cetaceans:

Swimmers should stay at least 30 m/100 feet from wild animals (it's up to the animal to come closer). Human and animal safety cannot be guaranteed and great caution should be exercized. If in doubt, retreat. Cetaceans and seals can occasionally be aggressive and attack. Operators may want clients to sign a special waiver before entering the water for any potential encounter. Ongoing research into the subject is continuing, see **www.wdcs.org** for more information and updates.

- Swimming or snorkeling only. No Scuba (except supervized ice diving). Do not enter the water within 30 m/100 ft. of the animals nor dive or jump in. Swim with gentle, quiet movements. Approach animals from the side and rear. Do not swim with calves of the year or pods with calves of the year. Vessels to maintain their normal distances.
- ARGENTINA: No swimming with cetaceans.
- NEW ZEALAND: No swimming with whales.
- BRAZIL: No swimming within 50 m/100 ft. of cetaceans.

2. SEALS
2a. General Guidelines:

Seals hauled out on land, rock or ice are sensitive to boats and human presence. Noises, smells and sights may elicit a reaction. When observing seals in water, please apply similar principles as outlined for cetaceans. On land, be aware of seal behaviour that indicates a seal has been disturbed.

- When viewing seals on ice or land, do not surround or separate them, especially mothers and pups. Stay on the side where they can see you.
- On beaches, avoid getting between seals and the sea, walk 'above' them.
- Try not to break their horizon.
- Do not feed them.
- Pups are often left alone when the mother is feeding. They are not abandoned and should be left alone and not touched.
- Keep commentary, conversation and engine noise to a minimum.
- Be aware of your radio volume.
- Any seal response other than a raised head should be avoided.
- Beware head raised and moving (open mouth in defense posture for Leopard Seal on ice, or Elephant Seal on land).
- If a seal dives, you should retreat.
- If a herd moves towards the water or there is a hurried entry into the water by many individuals, you should retreat.

Suggested minimum distances ashore 5–10 m (25 m from jousting bulls); New Zealand: 5 m. Beware of animals in tussock grass areas. Ideally, staff member should lead, carrying walking stick or equivalent.

2b. Swimming with Seals:
The suggestions for cetaceans apply. See 1h.

3. SEABIRDS
3a. General Guidelines:

- Birds such as penguins may be subject to disturbance by Zodiac operations close to landings or colonies.
- Approach or depart a landing or colony slowly to minimize any disturbance.
- Staff/crew should assess the best landing point – ideally as far from the birds as possible. This is particularly important if birds are molting near the shore.
- Avoid blocking 'walkways' in colonies and water entry and exit points. Avoid boat operations in water where birds enter and exit, are bathing, or are feeding close to colonies.
- Be aware of birds in the water and slow down and/or alter course to avoid any collision. Sometimes spectacular concentrations of seabirds may be found out at sea – rafts of birds either feeding on the surface, diving from it, or simply resting and bathing. Many of these birds may have flown hundreds if not thousands of miles, often to find food for their young.
- Stay on the fringes of these concentrations. Ships should stay 100 m and Zodiacs 30 m away.
- There may be occasions when swimming penguins find themselves in a Zodiac when they 'porpoise', landing

on the deck. Occupants should remain quiet and wait for the penguin to find its own way over the side and return to the water, normally by jumping onto the anchor box. It is normally not necessary to assist.

The same advice applies to 'feeding frenzies', which may involve species diving from the air into and under the surface of the sea.

- Some seabirds may be attracted to drifting vessels.
- Under no circumstances should 'chumming' (depositing fish guts or oil) occur to attract birds south of 60°.
- Never feed wild birds.
- Ashore, keep 5–10 m from nesting seabirds (10 m from nesting, 25 m from displaying Albatross on South Georgia). New Zealand allows approach to 5 m. Giant Petrels seem particularly prone to disturbance whilst nesting, stay 25–50 m away, if possible. If parent birds are blocked from returning to their nests, increased predation of eggs and chicks may occur by skuas and gulls.
- Take care in tussock grass where birds may be nesting, including in burrows under bare earth.
- If skuas (jaegers) or terns start dive-bombing, they are protecting young or nests. Retreat in the direction you approached from.

4. ENTANGLEMENT AND STRANDINGS

- Any animals entangled in fishing equipment, *etc.*, should be assisted where possible. Please use experienced staff/crew for these situations.
- Photographs of the entanglement should be taken. Please complete a report and send it to IAATO.

- Should you not be able to assist, please record details including Latitude and Longitude, species, and type of entanglement. Please report the event as soon as possible, so assistance may be sought from other vessels that may have experienced staff.
- Details of dead (floating) cetaceans and 'strandings' (beached) animals should be recorded. Where possible, please take photographs recording the front and side of the head of the animal (for species identification). Please include a scale of measurement (*e.g.* a ruler or Zodiac paddle) in the photographs.

5. IDENTIFICATION AND DATA COLLECTION

Identifying and, in many cases, recording species for triplog purposes is part of most onboard naturalists' remit. Logs, which include this data and the Latitude and Longitude of sightings, species identification and any additional information, such as identification photographs, are of immense value. Please send copies to the IAATO Secretariat **www.iaato.org**.

HELPFUL HINTS!

- Reducing Pollution from Engines – In all close wildlife encounters, please ensure you are using 'clean running' engines, especially on Zodiacs, and are creating minimum air and water pollution (*e.g.* light oil spills on the sea).
- Viewing Marine Animals – Polarizing sunglasses can considerably enhance viewing of submerged/partially submerged marine mammals in water.
- Encourage the use of binoculars for viewing marine mammals and seabirds.

ACKNOWLEDGEMENTS

Biologists and expedition staff who have worked many seasons in Antarctica helped to compile these Marine Animal Watching Guidelines:

IAATO Office of the Secretariat
E-mail: iaato@iaato.org
website: **www.iaato.org**

Whale watching regulations (as of 24/10/01):

Argentina Law 2381/84

Brazil IBAMA Edict 117 1996

Australia ANZECC Australian National Guidelines for Cetacean Observation 2000

New Zealand Marine Mammals Protection Regulations 1992

USA National Marine Fisheries Service Whale Watching Guidelines 1997

*Note: Vessel officers and staff should be aware of the full current regulations in place, in their respective operating areas.

Weddell Seal and pup

Adelie Penguin *Pygoscelis adeliae*
A common Antarctic penguin that has white underparts and a black back and head and lives and breeds in large exposed rookeries.

AGA
Full Face Mask.

Air Embolism
Blockage of blood stream by air bubbles. Can occur when air enters the bloodstream through ruptured alveoli. Can result in a block or disturbed blood flow to the body's tissues causing serious damage.

Algae
Any of various, chiefly aquatic, eukaryotic, photosynthetic organisms, ranging in size from single-celled forms to the Giant Kelp. Algae were once considered to be plants but are now classified separately because they lack true roots, stems, leaves, and embryos.

Alpha Flag
International maritime signal flag Alpha, meaning "Diver down, keep clear!" See Dive Flag.

Alternate Air Source
Any device a diver can use in place of the primary regulator, in order to make an ascent while still breathing normally.

Amphipod
A small crustacean of the order Amphipoda, such as the beach flea, having a laterally compressed body with no carapace.

Anemone
Any of numerous flowerlike marine coelenterates of the class Anthozoa, having a flexible cylindrical body and tentacles surrounding a central mouth.

Artificial Spit
See *Defogging solution*.

ASPA
Antarctic Specially Protected Area.

Atmosphere (ATA)
A unit of pressure roughly equal to the average atmospheric pressure at sea level on the earth. This pressure is reached at approximately 33 feet/10 m depth of sea water.

Back Roll Entry
Leaving the dive boat by sitting on its rail/pontoon and rolling backwards into the water.

Bar
One bar equals one atmosphere of pressure.

Barotrauma
Injury caused by unequal pressure between a space inside the body and the ambient pressure, or between two spaces within the body – usually caused by rapidly ascending.

Buoyancy Control Device (BCD)
Allows a diver to control their buoyancy under water by varying the volume of air inside its internal bladders. Also acts as a flotation device on the surface, and often doubles as a tank harness.

Bends
See *Decompression Sickness*.

Bergy Bits
Small, boulder size, pieces of floating ice that have broken off of an iceberg.

Booties
Neoprene fabric boots worn with open heel fins. For dry suits, this can also encompass a 'rock boot' – a hard boot at the foot of the dry suit.

Bottom Time
Generally the time between descending below the surface to the beginning of ascent.

Brash Ice
Accumulations of small floating fragments of ice, which can be from sea ice break up, chunks of iceberg, or glacial calving.

Brittle star
Common name for echinoderms belonging to the class Ophiuroidea. The name is derived from their habit of breaking off arms as a means of defense. Brittle stars can be distinguished from sea stars, or starfish, by their rounded central disk, sharply set off from the arms. Individuals are relatively small, usually less than 1 in. (2·5 cm) across the central disk, although the arms may be quite long.

Buddy
Diving partner.

Buddy Breathing
Two divers sharing air from one second stage.

Buoyancy
Upward force exerted by a fluid on any body immersed in it.

Buoyancy Compensator (BC)
See *BCD*.

BSAC
British Sub-Aqua Club.

C-Card
Divers Certification card issued by training organization to show your level of achievement.

Chinstrap Penguin *Pygoscelis antarctica*
A species of penguin found in the South Sandwich Islands, Antarctica, the South Orkneys, South Shetland, South Georgia, Bouvet Island, Balleny and Peter I Island. The name derives from the narrow black band under their chin which makes it appear as if they are wearing black helmets, making them one of the most easily identified types of penguin.

Chitin
Chitin, main constituent of the shells of arthropods. Chitin, a polysaccharide (see carbohydrate) analogous in chemical structure to cellulose, consists of units of a glucose derivative (N-acetyl-D-glucosamine) joined to form a long, unbranched chain. Like cellulose, chitin contributes strength and protection to the organism. In arthropods the chitinous shell, or exoskeleton, covers the surface of the body, does not grow, and is periodically cast off (molted). After the old shell is shed, a new, larger shell is secreted by the epidermis, providing room for future growth. The chitin is rigid except between some body segments and joints where it is thin and allows movement of adjacent parts.

Ctenopohores
Any of various marine animals of the phylum Ctenophora, having transparent, gelatinous bodies bearing eight rows of comblike cilia used for swimming.

Cylinder
Scuba tank or bottle.

DAN – Divers Alert Network
A non-profit organization exists to provide expert information and advice consistent with current literature for the benefit of the diving public.

DCS/DCI
See Decompression Sickness / Illness.

Decompression
Any change from one ambient pressure to a lower ambient pressure; always results in a reduction of gas pressures within the body.

Decompression Sickness / Illness (DCS/DCI)
Problems resulting from nitrogen bubbles leaving the body when ambient pressure is lowered *i.e.* ascending.

Defogging Solution
'Artificial Spit' that prevents fog from building up inside the mask during diving.

Dehydration
Reduced water content in the body – caused by diving without drinking enough water, too much alcohol the night before the dive, consuming diuretics, *etc.*

Demand Valve
Second stage valve of open circuit Scuba diving equipment, which opens when a breath is taken, allowing compressed air to flow into the mouth.

Depth Gauge
Device that indicates how deep you are, based on the ambient pressure.

Descent/Ascent Line
A line from a boat or buoy which can be used by divers to control their descent or ascent.

DIN Valve
Screwable alternative to a yoke fitting for first stage – commonly used in Europe, and for high pressure systems.

Dive Computer
A device that does all the dive calculations for you. It constantly calculates your nitrogen build-up, times, ascent rates, etc, for you before, during, and after the dive.

Dive Flag
Flag signaling divers in the water. Blue and white double tailed pennant, Code Flag Alpha (International), or a red rectangle with a diagonal white stripe (North America).

Dive Light
A light that you carry while diving. Some emit a very intense beam to illuminate the underwater arena, and some are lower intensity for location, as bright as a glow stick.

Dive Mask
A piece of equipment that covers your eyes and nose, allowing you to see underwater.

Dive Slate
A board, usually plastic, and pencil combination, that allows underwater communication.

Dive Tables
Various collections of dive times for specific depths, to guide the diver to stay within recommended safe limits for recreational diving.

Dragon Fish
A type of notothenid, often brightly colored with a long, flat head.

Dry Gloves
A form of diving glove attached or unattached to the dry suit, which allows the divers hands to stay dry throughout the dive.

Dry Suit
Water-tight suit that keeps the diver's body warm using air trapped within undergarments as the most important part of insulation – generally used in very cold waters.

Dual Regulator Systems
Dual regulator systems use two regulators on a single air supply to allow a diver to continue to access their air supply in the event of a malfunction in the primary regulator.

Encrusting Sponges
Sponges which have or begun to encased the outside of objects.

Environmentally Sealed
The addition of a chamber to the first stage of a regulator, which is surrounded by silicone or another unfreezing liquid. The chamber has a diaphragm or piston that transmits water pressure to the oil, so the first stage does its job with minimal freeze risk.

Equalization
Equalization is the act of forcing air into an open space to offset increasing hydrostatic pressure. This can be applied to such spaces as a dive mask or the diver's ears, and prevents what is known as a squeeze.

Eustachian Tube
Hollow structure of bone and cartilage extending from the middle ear to the rear of the throat. By permitting air to leave or enter the middle ear, the tube equalizes air pressure on either side of the eardrum.

First Stage
The part of the regulator which attaches to the Scuba tank valve and which is responsible for the first level of tank pressure reduction.

Fins
Worn on the feet to increase maneuverability and allow for faster swimming.

Free-flow
An uncontrolled expulsion of air from the second stage of a regulator.

FSW
Feet of Salt Water.

Full Face Mask
A piece of equipment that covers the entire face, encompassing both the second stage of the regulator and face mask.

Gastropod
Any of various mollusks of the class Gastropoda, such as the snail, slug, cowrie, or limpet, characteristically having a single, usually coiled shell or no shell at all, a ventral muscular foot for locomotion, and eyes and feelers located on a distinct head.

Gentoo Penguin *Pygoscelis papua*
A common penguin, easily recognized by the wide white stripe extending like a bonnet across the top of its head. Chicks have grey backs and white fronts. Adult Gentoos reach a height of 75–90 cm. They are the fastest penguin underwater, reaching speeds of 36 km/h.

Glacier
A huge mass of ice slowly flowing over a land mass, formed from compacted snow in an area where snow accumulation exceeds melting and sublimation.

Holdfast
The superficially root-like organ that attaches a seaweed or other alga, such as kelp, to a substrate.

Hood
A piece of material you wear over your head, and often your neck, while diving.

Horsecollar
Old style floatation device worn around the neck (replaced by the modern BCD).

HP Hose
High Pressure Hose, that goes from the regulator 1st stage to the air pressure gauge.

H-Valve
A tank valve with 2 outlets.

Humpback Whale *Megaptera novaeangliae*
A large marine mammal that belongs to the baleen whale suborder. It is well known for its breaching (leaping out of the water), its unusually long front fins, and its complex whale song.

Hydroid
Any of numerous characteristically colonial hydrozoan coelenterates having a polyp rather than a medusoid form as the dominant stage of the life cycle.

Hyperbaric Chamber
Air-tight chamber that can simulate the ambient pressure at depth – used for treating decompression illness.

Hypothermia
Hypothermia is a sudden and profound cooling of the temperature in the core of your body to below 35.5°C. This can have a crippling effect to the body. Continued cooling can result in an irregular heartbeat that can lead to death.

IAATO
International Association of Antarctic Tour Operators – a member organization founded in 1991 to advocate, promote and practice safe and environmentally responsible private-sector travel to the Antarctic.

Isopod
Any of the numerous crustaceans of the order Isopoda, characterized by a flattened body bearing seven pairs of legs, including the sow bugs and gribbles.

J-Valve
A valve that contains a spring-loaded mechanism that shuts off a diver's air supply when a certain tank pressure is reached.

K-Valve
A simple on/off valve, found on most dive cylinders.

Killer Whale *Orcinus orca*
A black-and-white predatory marine mammal that feeds on large fish, squid, and sometimes dolphins and seals. Also called Orca.

Leopard Seal *Hydrurga leptonyx*
A 'true seal' that is widely regarded as the most ferocious seal in the Antarctic. They feed on many other creatures, such as squid, King and Emperor Penguins, ocean fish, and Weddell Seals. Since the Leopard Seal is not very fast, it also relies on krill for much of its diet.

Limpet
A marine gastropod mollusk with a simple, flattened, conical shell. Certain species creep over rocks, feeding on algae when covered in water, but individuals return instinctively to their 'home' spot when the tide recedes. The muscular foot clings so powerfully that limpets are found in wave-swept areas where few other forms of life can survive.

Live Aboard
Dive boat with sleeping and eating facilities.

Log Book
Book in which to record completed dives. Includes dive time, depth, conditions, and remarks on each dive. Log books can be required on some charter dive boats.

LP Hose
Low-pressure hose. Runs from the regulator 1st stage to the 2nd stage or inflator.

Macaroni Penguin *Eudyptes chrysolophus*
A large, yellow-crested, black-and-white penguin, commonly found on South Georgia.

Manifold
Plumbing to connect 2 tanks so that one regulator can access gas in both tanks.

Mask Squeeze
Occurs during rapid descents if the diver neglects to equalize his or her mask. Blood-shot eyes are the most common symptom.

Minke Whale *Balaenoptera acutorostrata*
A small, dark gray baleen whale having a white underside and white bands on the flippers.

NASDS
National Association of Scuba Diving Schools.

NAUI
National Association of Underwater Instructors.

Nitrogen
Inert gas that makes up approximately 78% of air. It can cause physiological problems under pressure (*i.e.* nitrogen narcosis, decompression sickness).

Nitrogen Narcosis
Nitrogen narcosis develops with an increase in nitrogen partial pressure, anywhere from 3 atmospheres onwards. At this depth, nitrogen becomes dissolved in the lipids of the neurons, which interferes with signal transmission from neuron to neuron. Symptoms will increase dramatically with depth, and can lead to death.

NOAA

National Oceanic and Atmospheric Association of the U.S.A.

Notothenids

The dominant Antarctic fish species, occupying both sea bottom and water column ecological niches. Although lacking a swimbladder, they have undergone depth-related diversification, such as an increase in fatty tissues and a body density approaching neutral, to fill a variety of niches. As water temperatures average −1 to −4°C, Antarctic species have anitfreeze proteins in their blood.

O-ring

A flat or round ring made of rubber or plastic, used as a gasket in a variety of Scuba gear.

Octopus

Reserve 2nd stage regulator, with a long hose for buddy use.

Offgassing

Reducing the load of nitrogen (and/or other inert gasses) on the surface or on a safety stop. Also known as outgassing.

Oxygen

Gas vital to all life on this planet which makes up approximately 21% of air by volume. May cause physiological problems at high partial pressures.

Oxygen Toxicity

Damage or injury from inhaling too much oxygen. Dangerous if oxygen partial pressure exceeds 1·6 ATA – at around 64·6 m or 212 feet, using normal air. One of the first symptoms of oxygen toxicity while diving can be seizures.

PADI

Professional Association of Diving Instructors.

Pneumothorax

Abnormal presence of air in the pleural cavity potentially resulting in the collapse of the lung.

Pony Bottle

Small Scuba tanks strapped to your main dive gear. These tanks have their own first and second stages and can be used as an independent alternate air source.

Prescription Dive Mask

Special masks for divers needing refractive correction.

Pteropods

Any of various small marine gastropod mollusks of the subclass Opisthobranchia that have wing-like lobes on the feet. Also called sea butterfly.

Pulmonary Barotrauma

Rupture of the lung surface from increased pressure of ascent from depth.

Purge Valve

Purge valves allow masks and regulators to be cleared easily without having to remove the mask from the diver's face or the regulator from the diver's mouth.

Pycnogonids

See **Sea Spider**.

Recreational Scuba Diving (RSD)

Diving to prescribed limits, including a depth no greater than 40 m or 130 feet, using only compressed air and never requiring a decompression stop.

Regulator

Regulators reduce the highly compressed tank gas to ambient pressure to allow a diver to breath underwater. Comprised of first and second stage valves.

Reverse Block

When the internal pressure of an air space is greater than the external pressure, which can create a problem upon accent.

Reverse Squeeze

Pain or discomfort in an enclosed space (*e.g.* sinuses, middle ear, inside mask) on ascent from a dive – See **Reverse Block**.

RIB

Rigid Inflatable Boat – generally with solid hull and deck and large inflatable tubes.

ROV

Remotely Operated Vehicle.

Safety Stop

Generally 3–5 minutes spent at 3–6 m for the purpose of off-gassing as an extra safety precaution. Is by definition not mandatory for safe ascent from the dive. See decompression stop.

Safety Sausage

A brightly colored, plastic inflatable tube that stands about 3 m or 10 feet out of the water. It can also be laid flat on the water to signal aircraft. It is inflatable by regulator, or orally, and after each use can be deflated and rolled up to fit into a BCD pocket.

Save-A-Dive Kit
A small box that contains tools and spare parts for diving equipment. This is for on the spot repairs of minor problems, such as O-ring replacement or regulator tightening.

Sea Cucumber
Marine animal (echinoderm) with an elongated body and leathery skin that lives on the sea bed. Although they have reduced body armor in the form of a calcified shell, sea cucumbers often have protuberances that function to look like armor. Other species are camouflaged so as to look like rocks and other surfaces underwater.

Sea Urchin
Spherical-shaped marine echinoderm with movable spines covering the body. The body wall is a firm, globose shell, or test, made of fused skeletal plates and marked by regularly arranged tubercles to which the spines are attached. They feed on all kinds of plant and animal material and occur in all seas and at all depths, but prefer shallower waters and rocky bottoms.

Scooter
Diver Propulsion Vehicle.

Scour Zone
The area, generally above 10 m, that is battered by ice, creating a limited benthic community.

SCUBA
Self-Contained Underwater Breathing Apparatus.

Sea Star (Starfish)
Any of various marine echinoderms of the class Asteroidea, characteristically with a thick, often spiny, body with five arms extending from a central disk.

Sea Spider
Common name for members of the class Pycnogonida, long-legged, rather spiderlike organisms of the phylum Chelicerata, widely distributed in marine waters. Most are tiny, 1–9 mm (0·04–0·36 in.), and live in littoral regions, crawling about over the surface of sessile animal colonies or seaweeds. Some live on or in clams. There are deep-sea forms, some becoming quite large; *Colossendeis colossea* has a leg span of nearly 2 ft (60 cm). Members of this class are relatively common and widely distributed; well over 400 species are known.

Second Stage
The part of the regulator you put into your mouth to breathe through. See **Demand Valve**.

Sessile Jellyfish
Jellyfish that have attached themselves to a stationary object and remain stationary themselves.

Sinuses
Air spaces within the skull that are in contact with ambient pressure through openings in the back of the nasal passages.

Sinus Squeeze
Occurs during a rapid descent when a diver is unable to equalize the air space in the sinus cavity. A diver experiencing sinus squeeze will often experience pain and surface with blood in his or her mask due to the trauma caused by a squeeze.

Sinusitis
Inflammation or infection of the sinuses.

Snorkel
Breathing device consisting of a bent tube fitting into a swimmer's mouth and extending above the surface – allows swimmer to breathe while face down in the water.

SPG
Submersible Pressure Gauge, indicating tank pressure.

Sponge
Any of numerous aquatic, chiefly marine, invertebrate animals of the phylum Porifera, characteristically having a porous skeleton composed of fibrous material or siliceous or calcareous spicules and often forming irregularly shaped colonies attached to an underwater surface.

Squeeze
Pain of discomfort in an enclosed space (sinuses, middle ears, inside a mask) caused by shrinkage of that space – occurs on descent.

SSI
Scuba Schools International.

Surface Marker Buoy
Buoy with a flag and a line to a diver below, to indicate position to surface vessels.

Tank Light
A light attached to a divers tank while night diving, or in poorly lighted sites, to let other divers know their position.

Thermocline
Sudden changes in water temperature with changing depth. They occur when warmer, lighter water forms a layer above a denser, colder layer of water. If

strongly affected by currents it can be the other way round occasionally.

Tunicate
Any of various chordate marine animals of the subphylum Tunicata or Urochordata having a cylindrical or globular body enclosed in a tough outer covering; includes the sea squirts and salps.

Vertigo
Dizziness brought on by the inequality of pressures in the inner ear, as well as a variety other diving related accidents, such as Oxygen toxicity and **DCI**.

Visibility
The distance a diver can see underwater measured in feet or meters.

Weddell Seal *Leptonychotes weddellii*
A 'true seal' named after Sir James Weddell, commander of British sealing expeditions in the Weddell Sea. They occur in large numbers and inhabit the circumpolar region of the southern hemisphere, including Antarctica.

Wet Suit
A close-fitting garment made of a neoprene that is worn by divers to retain body heat by trapping a warm layer of water next to the skin.

Wooly Bear
A thick undergarment for a dry suit. Named for the original material from which it was made; nowadays synthetic fabrics are used.

Worms
Any of various invertebrates, as those of the phyla Annelida, Nematoda, Nemertea, or Platyhelminthes, having a long, flexible, rounded or flattened body, often without obvious appendages.

Y-Valve
A tank valve with two outlets.

Zodiac
Brand name inflatable boat or **RIB**.

Antarctic Limpet *Nacella concinna*

PHOTO AND ART CREDITS

Cover: Cotton Coulson and Sisse Brimberg
Dedication *Dennis Cornejo and Lisa Eareckson Kelley*: Tracy Shea
P8 *Martin Enckell*: Henrik Enckell
P11 *Lemaire Channel*: Lisa Eareckson Kelley
P14 *Divers in Antarctica*: Martin Enckell
P16 *Ushuaia*: Lisa Eareckson Kelley
P25 TOP: *Weddell Seal*:; MIDDLE: *Anemone*; BOTTOM: *Sea star*: Lisa Eareckson Kelley
P26 *Leopard Seal*: Lisa Eareckson Kelley
P27–30 *Leopard Seal taking Emperor Penguin*: Deborah Harris
P31 *Leopard Seal*: Mattieu Meur/Waterproof Expeditions
P33 *Leopard Seal and diver*: Göran Ehlmé
P34 *Leopard Seal Project Logo*: Ian Bullock
P34 *Leopard Seal and Zodiac*: Roger Munns / Scubazoo
P36 *Anemone*: Lisa Eareckson Kelley
P37 *Dragon Fish*: Lisa Eareckson Kelley
P38 LEFT: *Unidentified sponge*; RIGHT: *Tunicate and Brittle star*: Lisa Eareckson Kelley
P39 TOP: *Gastropod*; BOTTOM: *Nudibranch*: Lisa Eareckson Kelley
P40 *Diver using video*: Lisa Eareckson Kelley
P41 TOP LEFT: *Bivalve*; TOP RIGHT: *Scrumming stars*: Lisa Eareckson Kelley; BOTTOM: *Leopard Seal and Gentoo Penguin*: Göran Ehlmé
P42 TOP: *Flying the ROV*; BOTTOM: *Deploying the ROV*: Tim Soper
P44 LEFT: *Sea star*; RIGHT: *Sea cucumber*: Lisa Eareckson Kelley
P45 TOP RIGHT: *Brittle star*: Lisa Eareckson Kelley TOP LEFT: *Sea urchin*: Martin Enckell BOTTOM: *Limpet*: Lisa Eareckson Kelley
P46 TOP: *Sea urchin with 'hats'*; MIDDLE: *Nudibranch*; BOTTOM: *Nudibranch*: Lisa Eareckson Kelley
P47 *Tunicate*: Lisa Eareckson Kelley
P48 TOP: *Worm*; BOTTOM: *Nemertean worm*: Lisa Eareckson Kelley
P49 TOP: *Nothothenid fish*; BOTTOM: *Young notothenid*: Lisa Eareckson Kelley
P50 TOP: *Sea anemone*; BOTTOM: *Soft coral*: Lisa Eareckson Kelley
P51 *Sponge growth*: Lisa Eareckson Kelley
P52 TOP: *Kelp*; BOTTOM: *Sea spider*: Lisa Eareckson Kelley
P53 TOP: View toward Eichorst Island : Bill J. Baker BOTTOM: Sea life below the surface: Bill J. Baker
P54 TOP LEFT: *Amphipods grazing*: Bill J. Baker TOP RIGHT: *A lone amphipod*: Bill J. Baker BOTTOM LEFT: *Latrunculia apicalis*: Bill J. Baker BOTTOM RIGHT: *Odontaster* sp.: Bill J. Baker

P55 Palmerolide and nudibranch: Bill J. Baker
P56 TOP LEFT: *Austrodoris* nudibranchs: Bill J. Baker TOP RIGHT: Frilly Nudibranch: Bill J. Baker BOTTOM LEFT: *Clione antarctica*: Bill J. Baker BOTTOM RIGHT: *Limicina limicina*: Bill J. Baker
P57 TOP: Blackfin Icefish: Bill J. Baker BOTTOM: Candelabrum penola: Bill J. Baker
P59 Antarctic map: derived from *Antarctic Wildlife* (Princeton WILD*Guides*) based on maps 13A and 13B courtesy of BAS
P60 *Point Wild*: Tim Soper
P61 TOP LEFT: *Undescribed anemone*: Lisa Eareckson Kelley MIDDLE LEFT: *Encrusting sponge*; BOTTOM LEFT: *Anemone*; TOP RIGHT: *Encrusting sponge*: David Cothran video stills; BOTTOM RIGHT: *Sea spider*: David Cothran video still
P62 *Landscape*: Lisa Eareckson Kelley
P63 TOP LEFT: *Notothenid*; BOTTOM LEFT: *Sea star*; TOP RIGHT: *Anemone*; BOTTOM RIGHT: *Sea urchin*: Lisa Eareckson Kelley
P65 TOP LEFT: *Weddell Seal*: Lisa Eareckson Kelley BOTTOM LEFT: *Ice*: David Cothran video still TOP RIGHT: *The hut on Paulet Island*: Lisa Eareckson Kelley; BOTTOM RIGHT: *Scour zone*: Lisa Eareckson Kelley
P66 *Sponge*: Lisa Eareckson Kelley and Dennis Cornejo video still
P67 TOP: *Amphipod*; MIDDLE LEFT: *Limpet*; MIDDLE CENTER: *Comb jelly*; MIDDLE RIGHT: *Crinoid and urchin*: Lisa Eareckson Kelley and Dennis Cornejo video stills; BOTTOM: *Crinoid and urchin*: David Cothran video still
P68 *Tunicate*: Lisa Eareckson Kelley
P69 TOP LEFT: *Nototheni*; BOTTOM LEFT: *Soft Coral*; TOP RIGHT: *Ctenophore*; BOTTOM RIGHT: *The wall*: Lisa Eareckson Kelley
P70 TOP RIGHT: *Colonial salp*: Lisa Eareckson Kelley and Dennis Cornejo video still
P71 *Ctenophore*: David Cothran video still MIDDLE RIGHT: *Polychete worm*: Lisa Eareckson Kelley BOTTOM RIGHT: *Pteropod*: Lisa Eareckson Kelley and Dennis Cornejo video still BOTTOM LEFT: *Sea cucumber*: Lisa Eareckson Kelley
P72 TOP LEFT: *Brittle star*; TOP RIGHT: *Sea star*: Lisa Eareckson Kelley BOTTOM: *Sea urchins*: Lisa Eareckson Kelley and Dennis Cornejo video still
P73 BOTTOM: *Notothenid*: Martin Enckell
P76 *Sea cucumber*: Lisa Eareckson Kelley

SUGGESTED FURTHER READING

Billings, Henry. 1956. *Man Underwater.* Littleworth Press London.

Brueggeman, Peter. 2003. *Diving Under Antarctic Ice: A History.* Scripps Institute of Oceanography.

Burton, Robert and John Croxall. 2012. *A Field Guide to the Wildlife of South Georgia.* Princeton University Press.

Carwardine, Mark. 2002. *Whales Dolphins and Porpoises.* Dorling Kindersley.

de Latil, Pierrre and Rivoire, Jean. 1954. *Man and the Underwater World.* Jarrolds Publishers London Ltd.

Gurney, Alan. 2000. *The Race to the White Continent: Voyages to the Antarctic.* W. W. Norton and Company.

Heacox, Kim. 1999. *Shackelton: The Antarctic Challenge.* National Geographic Publishing.

Lowen, James. 2011. *Antarctic Wildlife: A Visitor's Guide.* Princeton University Press.

National Science Foundation. 1995. *Geographic Names of the Antarctic.* National Science Foundation.

Poncet, Sally and Kim Crosbie. 2012. *A Visitor's Guide to South Georgia.* Princeton University Press.

Rosove, Michael H. 2000. *Let Hero's Speak: Antarctic Explorers, 1772–1922.* Naval Institute Press.

Rubin, Jeff. 2000. *Lonely Planet Antarctica.* Lonely Planet Publications.

Shirihai, Hadoram. 2002. *The Complete Guide to Antarctic Wildlife.* Alula Press.

Soper, Tony. 2000. *Antarctica: A Guide to Wildlife.* Bradt.

Stonehouse, Bernard. 2000. *The Last Continent: Discovering Antarctica.* SCP Books.

Stonehouse, Bernard. 2002. *Encyclopedia of Antarctica and the Southern Oceans.* Wiley.

Todd, Frank S. 2004. *Birds, Mammals of the Antarctic, Subantarctic, and Falkland Island.* Ibis Publishing Co.

Trewby, Mary. 2002. *Antarctica: An Encyclopedia from Abbott Ice Shelf to Zooplankton.* Firefly Books Ltd.

ABOUT THE AUTHOR

Lisa Eareckson Kelley grew up alongside the great lakes, and attended Northern Michigan University. Graduating *Summa Cum Laude* with a bachelor's degree in health education and human biology, Lisa completed postgraduate work in immunology before a radical career change took her to sea aboard Lindblad Expeditions' *Endeavour*. Working as Expedition Leader, Undersea Specialist and Divemaster, have taken Lisa from the remote islands of the Mid-Atlantic Ridge to Europe, as well as both coasts of South America and the Azores. However, it is the extreme wilderness of the Polar Regions that she finds most rewarding, and Lisa spends much of her year exploring the Antarctic Peninsula, Sub-Antarctic Islands, and the Arctic. She has also participated in expeditions by icebreaker to Antarctica's Weddell and Ross Seas, as well as the High Russian Arctic archipelago of Franz Josef Land. Probably the first person to learn to dive in the Antarctic, Lisa completed her first open water dive at Cape Horn before continuing south to complete her training in the waters of the Antarctic Peninsula. She holds NAUI Divemaster certification, has combined her medical training to become an IMCA Diver Medical Technician, and continues to spend the austral summers in the Antarctic, diving at every opportunity.

Göran Ehlmé originates from Sweden and has planned and led many expeditions to the polar regions, and was the first to lead diving expeditions to the Arctic and Antarctic. He has over 30 years diving experience and dives both open water and under the ice, being particularly experienced with Walrus, Emperor Penguins, and Leopard Seals. As an underwater cameraman, Göran has been on assignment filming documentaries for Animal Planet, the BBC, Canal Plus, and National Geographic. He won the BBC's Shell Wildlife Photographer of the Year 2006 award. Göran is also the founder and head-designer of the Waterproof dive suits, neoprene dry suits, wet suits and accessories.   **www.waterproof.se | www.waterproof-expeditions.com**

Shona Muir undertook a 12-month research project investigating interactions between Leopard Seals and humans. This research was sponsored and promoted by the Kirsty Brown Fund and supported by the British Antarctic Survey. Shona has a background in social / humanistic research and Antarctic diving research. She completed her BA (Hons) in Social Geography and undertook fieldwork and academic study on Antarctic diving through the University of Canterbury's Gateway Antarctica program in New Zealand.

Dr. Dennis Cornejo began Scuba diving during the mid-1970s as part of a sea turtle research project. After concluding his research on sea turtles in the mid-1980s, Dennis enjoyed recreational diving while pursuing various terrestrial research programs. Among them: the community ecology of desert toads and their tadpoles for a master's degree at the University of Arizona, at Tucson; and the morphology and biogeography of giant North American cacti for a doctorate in botany at the University of Texas, at Austin. In the mid-1990s, Dennis became a diving professional, qualifying as a NAUI Instructor, and has now dived around the world.

Dr. Bill J. Baker took his first academic appointment at the Florida Institute of Technology, where he began studies of natural products and chemical ecology of Antarctic marine organisms. Diving at McMurdo Station, Dr. Baker and long-time collaborator Dr. James B. McClintock conducted ecological studies of Antarctic marine natural products. In 2000, Dr. Charles D. Amsler joined the team to lead the studies of the algal dominated environs of Palmer Station. Dr. Baker now serves as Director of the Center for Drug Discovery and Innovation where much of the chemistry found in collected samples is studied for its potential to improve human health.

Martin Enckell is Swedish-born and began his career at sea at a young age. Since that time he has successfully combined a love of nature and the water, travelling all over the world working as Zodiac Driver and Dive Master and Guide in the Arctic, including the North Pole, and from Australia through Europe to the West Indies. Wanting to specialize in the colder waters of the world he worked in Antarctica as Expedition Leader, Zodiac Driver, and with his brother Henrik, and has guided diving on the Peninsula, South Georgia and the Falkland Islands. Martin is a qualified PADI Instructor and HSE Safety Diver.

Henrik Enckell is a Swedish dive instructor with PADI and NAUI, an IANTD Trimix and Rebreather diver and he also holds a Masters degree in electrical engineering. His diving career started in the Red Sea and today he mainly dives deep wrecks in the Baltic Sea using a mixed gas closed circuit rebreather. Henrik is a Dive Guide and Zodiac Driver in Antarctica. He has a military background and has served with both UN and NATO in peacekeeping operations in the Middle East and former Yugoslavia. When he is not diving he is taking care of his three daughters.